Frau De[...] [danc-]
ers and me[...] [he-]ard
music and [...] first
act. We were in the [...] was
really nervous. What if I did something
wrong in front of all those people? My hands
began to sweat, but I was afraid to dry them
on my costume.

Around me, the other dancers began to
do limbering-up exercises. That was a good
idea, I thought; it would keep me from thinking about making a mistake. I limbered up
with unusual enthusiasm until Frau Dertl
came, wished everyone good luck, and herded
us into the wings.

The music began and I listened carefully
for my cue. I could feel my heart beating. I
was scared to death, and wished that I was
anyplace but where I was. And then I heard
my cue! My legs began to tingle. I took a few
steps to center stage.

Then, to the Johann Strauss waltz, I
danced what I had been rehearsing for so
long. I knew my legs were going higher than
they had when I had practiced with Frau
Dertl. And it seemed to me that my position
on *pointe* was much more steady than it had
ever been.

The music stopped. There was loud applause. All those people were applauding *me*!
I was in heaven!

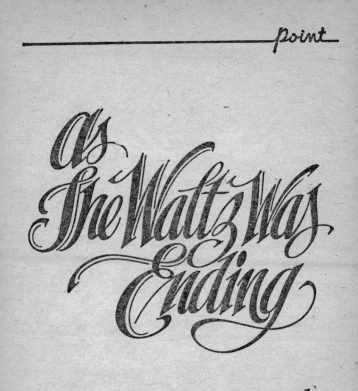

As The Waltz Was Ending

Emma Macalik Butterworth

SCHOLASTIC INC.
New York Toronto London Auckland Sydney

ISBN 0-590-33210-4

Copyright © 1982 by Emma Macalik Butterworth. All rights reserved. Published by Scholastic Inc., 730 Broadway, New York, NY 10003, by arrangement with Macmillan Publishing Co., Inc.

12 11 10 9 8 7 6 5 4 3 2 1   5   5 6 7 8 9/8 0/9

Printed in the U.S.A.   01

For Bill
without whom this book
would never have been written.

As The Waltz Was Ending

Part One

Chapter 1

A photograph taken that long-ago day has somehow survived. Not a Polaroid, for instant photography was yet to be invented. Not even color. Just a black-and-white photograph taken one sunny day before Vienna's St. Stephen's Cathedral by a man who made his living with his small camera.

He asked if he could take the picture by aiming his camera at his intended subjects. If they stopped and smiled, he took the picture, then handed the people he had photographed a coupon. The coupon gave his name and address and listed his prices. If you filled in your name and address and sent him the money, a week or so later the postman would deliver your photograph.

The photograph shows an eight-year-old girl in her confirmation dress. She is holding the candle she carried up the aisle during the ceremony. Her aunt, her sponsor, in her Sunday best clothing, is holding the little girl's hand. The photograph is over forty years old, and cracked and faded brown. You can still see, however, that the little girl, wearing her blond hair in braids, is smiling broadly; that all is right with her world.

That day is much more clear in my memory than the photograph, for I was that little girl who had her picture taken on her Confirmation Day.

Confirmation, acceptance into the Roman Catholic Church, was an event of enormous importance in the life of a middle-class child in Vienna in 1935. Austria is a Roman Catholic country. Vienna's St. Stephen's Cathedral is her most famous landmark, even more famous than the Vienna State Opera.

I had gone all year to Catechism class at my parish church. My catechist, Father Kovac, a pleasant elderly priest, stern only when I hadn't paid attention, had finally said I was ready for the biggest day in the life of a Roman Catholic girl.

In order to understand what the priest was saying during Mass, I had had to learn some Latin. I had learned that when the priest said *"Dominus vobiscum"* (The Lord be with you), I was to respond with *"Et cum spiritu tuo"* (And with your spirit).

Father Kovac would have been less pleased with me if he had known the real reason I was so happy to be about to be confirmed.

On Good Friday an open casket with a life-sized, uncomfortably lifelike effigy of Jesus Christ was set up in the side aisle of my parish church. His eyes were closed. He had a gray beard down to his shoulders, and was dressed in a gray robe with his long toes sticking out the bottom of the robe.

My father had told me over and over that it wasn't really Jesus Christ in there, but only a wax dummy. It didn't look like a dummy to me. I was terrified of it when the priests and nuns marched me and the other unconfirmed children past it.

I would happily have given up a new Easter outfit, and the Easter parade, if I didn't have to walk past Jesus Christ in his casket, but the only way to get out of it was to be confirmed. Now I was about to be confirmed and freed from the annual march past that frightening casket.

Confirmation carried with it certain other temporal pleasures, and thinking of these had kept me awake long after the time I was normally asleep the night before Confirmation Day.

We lived on Esterhazygasse, in the Sixth District near the center of Vienna, in a Renaissance-style apartment building built more than a century earlier. It was sheathed in gray marble to the level of the first floor and above that the five-story building was of yellow brick. It was imposing, even majestic, built along with thousands of similar buildings during the Belle Epoque of the Austro-Hungarian Empire, when Emperor Franz Josef ruled over an empire second in size and power only to the British Empire.

Inside, huge, double wooden doors opened

into the lobby, and a wide staircase climbed four floors. Each floor had three large and comfortable apartments laid out in much the same way. Our apartment, like the others, had a long, L-shaped entrance hall. Four doors to the left, and three doors to the right, opened off it. On the left, the kitchen, the bathroom, my room, and the guest room had windows facing the courtyard. On the right, the living room, the dining room, and my parents' bedroom faced the street.

The kitchen was large and airy. The breakfast table sat by the window, surrounded by flower pots on stands. More flower pots were on the windowsill. The kitchen floor was linoleum. All the other rooms had polished hardwood floors and Oriental rugs. A corner of each room held a brightly colored porcelain-over-cast-iron coal stove shaped something like a steeple where the pointed tops almost reached the high ceilings.

The apartment had been a wedding present from my father's parents when he married my mother ten years earlier. The building had then just gone through remodeling, and was in effect a "new" house.

Singing birds woke me up on my Confirmation Day and I got out of bed and went to the windows of my bedroom. When I pushed the curtains aside, the bright sunlight hurt my eyes.

I climbed onto the wide marble windowsill and reached for the knob in the center of the tall, narrow, old-fashioned windows. I was always afraid that I would slip, crash through the windows, and fall two floors to the cobblestones of the courtyard.

I pushed the double windows outward, and fitted the long, round metal rods on their bottoms into small holes in the windowsill to hold the windows open.

It was very quiet. The only sound came from the birds in the two huge chestnut trees. Under them, the lilac bushes had just begun to bud.

Petja, my wire-haired fox terrier, jumped up onto the windowsill and barked at the birds in the trees.

And then the doorbell rang and I wondered who had come to call so early in the morning. I turned from the window and started to get dressed.

Marcella, my best friend, opened the door while I was still braiding my hair.

"What're you doing here so early?" I asked.

"This is from Olaf and me," Marcella said. She handed me a small, round bouquet of tiny pink rosebuds, held together with a pink velvet ribbon. Olaf was Marcella's brother, five years older than we girls and our reluctant sometime chaperone.

"They're exactly the same color as my new dress!" I exclaimed in delight.

"I know. Your mother told me."

I ran into the kitchen to show the bouquet to my father, who was having his breakfast. He told me how lucky I was to have a friend like Marcella. I knew I was. My father then asked Marcella if she had had breakfast. She shook her head no.

He pointed to my chair and told her to sit down. I was to be denied breakfast: Taking anything but a glass of water before receiving Communion was considered a sin.

My mother put the coffee pot and a pitcher of warm milk on the table. Both were white china, decorated with painted flowers. She and I liked a lot of milk and sugar in our coffee, and she warmed the milk to keep the mixture hot. My father offered Marcella a rattan basket of freshly baked, still warm *Kaisersemmeln* (Emperor rolls). Each of them took a roll, cut it in half, and spread butter and marmalade on it. I desperately wished that I could have just one, too.

The rolls were delivered still hot from the oven early every morning by a bakery boy who wore a baker's uniform of white jacket, trousers, huge apron, and a stiffly starched white hat. He carried a huge white cloth-covered rattan basket through the building, leaving the day's rolls in a white cloth bag hanging from a string the housewives put outside their doorknobs at night.

The doorbell rang again. This time it was my Aunt Anna, my father's sister and my sponsor for the confirmation ceremony. She was wearing a flowing light blue dress, with a huge, round stiff lace hat and long, up-to-her-elbows gloves of the same color.

"You look absolutely gorgeous, Anna," my father said to her. I thought so, too.

"Thank you, Josef," Aunt Anna replied, obviously pleased with the compliment from her youngest brother. "But Emmy is the beauty today. A genuine Viennese doll."

"She does look pretty, doesn't she?" he said proudly. I beamed. I wasn't that used to compliments.

"I'm sorry Otto couldn't come," Aunt Anna said.

My Uncle Otto Schober, Aunt Anna's husband, who was second-chair violinist in the Vienna Opera orchestra, was to have been my second sponsor. I already knew he wouldn't be going with us to St. Stephen's Cathedral. There was a matinee at the Opera and he had to play. In Vienna, everything is secondary to music, and all other music is secondary to what is going on at the Opera.

I was secretly glad that he wouldn't be there. I thought that Uncle Otto was a cold man. I knew he seldom laughed or was really nice to anyone, not even to his son, my cousin Fritz. I had heard my father tell my mother that he didn't think Otto liked anybody at the Opera either. So far as I knew, he didn't like anyone in the Macalik family. He was my sponsor only because my parents had been Fritz's sponsors when he had been confirmed eight years before.

Viennese Catholics take being a sponsor seriously. Aunt Anna had frequently checked to see how well I was coming along with my catechist and took my upcoming confirmation and First Communion at least as seriously as I did.

I went to my room and pushed aside my school uniforms to get at my new pink confirmation dress. Most of the time, like all Catholic girls in Vienna, I wore school uniforms. The warm-weather uniform, a pretty plaid cotton jumper worn with knee-length white stockings, wasn't too bad. But I hated the winter uniform, a dark blue woolen jumper worn over heavy woolen gray stockings. I hated the way it looked, and I hated the way it itched.

My confirmation dress was the prettiest dress I had ever owned. I would be nearly as pretty as Aunt Anna when we went, alone, to St. Stephen's. Parents weren't welcome. On Confirmation Day, confirmation children belonged to their sponsors. It was a two-way street: Sponsors were expected to provide the confirmation dress (or suit, for a boy), a prayer book, a wristwatch, and a day on the town to mark the acceptance of the confirmation child into the Holy Catholic Church.

Aunt Anna took my hand as we left the apartment and my parents and Marcella followed us down the stairs to the ground floor foyer.

A coachman and a *Fiaker* drawn by two white horses waited for us outside. Riding to St. Stephen's Cathedral in a horse-drawn carriage was as much a part of the First Communion ritual as the prayer book and wristwatch. The roof of the *Fiaker* had been folded back. Above the seats was a wire arch covered with dainty pink artificial flowers (fresh flowers would have wilted in the sun). There were flowers on both sides of the carriage and on the spokes of the wheels. The coachman wore pink flowers on the side of his top hat and in his lapel. Even his whip had a flower on its tip. (Coachmen seldom whipped their horses; the whip was mostly for decoration.) Still more pink flowers decorated the horses' harness and blinders.

My aunt boosted me up into the *Fiaker*, and the coachman smiled at me, lifted his top hat, and snapped the reins. The horses began to move. My parents and Marcella waved and yelled "Good-bye, good-bye!" until the *Fiaker* turned around a corner.

The *Fiaker* took us past my parish church on Mariahilferstrasse, a broad avenue leading through the Sixth Mariahilf Bezirk. Vienna has twenty-four Bezirke (sections), laid out in a circle. The First Bezirk, "The Inner City," is in the center of the city, surrounded by the Ringstrasse. Each section is numbered, but is generally referred to by name. Mariahilferstrasse begins at the Ring, a wide boulevard lined with chestnut trees, which circles the first section. On or within the Ring are many of Vienna's most imposing buildings, including the Parliament, the Opera, the Courthouse, museums, the University, the former Imperial Winter Palace, a dozen other former palaces, and, in the center, St. Stephen's Cathedral. At the Ring the

Fiaker turned right toward the Opera House. I told my aunt I could imagine the Emperor and other noblemen riding in their *Fiakers*, seeing the same trees and buildings we were seeing.

The *Fiaker* turned left off the Ring onto Kärntnerstrasse, Vienna's Fifth Avenue, which runs from the Ring to St. Stephen's Place.

The service was to begin at eleven. We were fifteen minutes early. There were so many other *Fiakers* in front of us that it took ten minutes before we finally reached the ornate, giant portal of the cathedral.

The coachman climbed down from his high seat, walked around the *Fiaker*, and opened the little side door. The cathedral bell, the twenty-ton *Pummerin*, began to boom. (The bell, named after the deep booming sound it makes, was cast from melted-down Turkish brass cannon captured when the Turks failed to capture Vienna in the seventeenth century.) The coachman held out his hand to Aunt Anna and helped her, and then me, out of the carriage.

We entered the cathedral and walked down the red-carpeted aisle. There were altars on both sides of the cathedral. They looked small in the huge cathedral, but each was actually about as large as the Mariahilfer parish church. Mounted on the walls, and on the cathedral's pillars, twenty feet off the marble floor, were life-sized statues of long-dead popes, cardinals, and other churchmen.

The main alter, way up in front, looked as if it had been dipped in gold, and a sea of four-foot-tall candles surrounded the altar with as many baskets of flowers between them. A huge stone Crucifix hung on the wall behind the altar.

One of the many priests circulating through the cathedral showed us to a pew halfway to the altar.

After a while the *Pummerin* stopped its deep booming. It was eerily silent in the cathedral for a moment and then the enormous pipe organ came to life, joined a moment later by a hundred-man-plus choir. The sound, echoing off the walls, was awesome, almost frightening.

The music and the choir now became even louder. People in the pews stood up, and Aunt Anna and I joined them.

A priest came down the aisle carrying a large cross, followed by another priest in an ornate, golden robe. My aunt whispered to me that he was the bishop who would confirm me.

Behind him in the procession were at least a dozen more monsignori, priests, and deacons. Then came the ministrants, boys who had a role in the ceremony, dressed in long red robes under white lace blouses. The ministrants passed by slowly, waving little golden bowls of smoking, exotic incense on long chains.

When the last ministrant had reached the altar, the priest who had shown us to our pew signaled for me to go to the aisle. My aunt put a long white candle, decorated with dainty silk lilies of the valley and a long white ribbon, into my hand: my First Communion candle. Priests walked between the girls and boys in the aisle and lit the candles.

The bishop at the altar, raising his voice so as to be heard all over, said, *"Dominus vobiscum."*

"Et cum spiritu tuo," a hundred young voices replied.

The bishop went to the container for the host, took out the golden chalice containing the Communion bread, and placed it on the altar. When he had consecrated the bread and wine, he picked up the chalice and a host (actually a small piece of unleavened bread) and carried them to one of the priests. The bishop dipped the host into the wine, and then put it into the priest's mouth. It was exactly the way the priest gave Communion in my parish church and I realized that soon I would receive Holy Communion the same way as the priest had.

The line of children and their sponsors in front of me began to move. Soon I was on my knees before the altar, with my aunt standing behind me. The bishop laid his hands on my head and said something in Latin. Then he removed his hands and moved to the next child. A priest came up and served me my First Communion. The host was dry and I was afraid I wouldn't be able to swallow it, but it melted quickly in my mouth.

Then Aunt Anna touched my shoulder as a signal to get up, and we returned to the pew. When the last of the children and their sponsors had returned to their pews, the organ music and the choir stopped, and the bell began to boom again. I was sure it rang for me alone.

Outside the cathedral I blew out the candle, to be kept as a souvenir, and waited for our *Fiaker* to appear in the long line.

A commercial photographer with several cameras hanging around his neck came up to us. He made a bargain with my aunt for pictures, which would be mailed to us.

The religious part of my First Communion Day was over. Now it was time for the earthly celebration.

The horses' hooves on the cobblestones made a pleasant "clup, clup, clup" sound. When people saw the flowered-bedecked *Fiaker*, they stopped and waved at the confirmed and her sponsor, and we waved back.

Aunt Anna put two small, gift-wrapped boxes into my lap and I opened the long, thin one first. It contained a silver wristwatch with the date and my initials engraved on the back.

I was happy to finally have a real watch. Marcella had had a watch as long as I had known her, since we had started school together, and she wasn't even confirmed. She had told me that Protestants didn't think watches had anything to do with confirmation.

The package shaped like a book contained the expected prayer book.

We drove to the Prater, Vienna's two-thousand-acre park near the Danube. Chestnut trees on both sides of the avenue leading to the amusement park (which had the world's largest Ferris wheel) were in full bloom and looked like white Christmas trees. Some Confirmation *Fiakers* had beaten us there and more were behind us.

Our first stop was the amusement park. My aunt told the driver we would be at least two hours, and gave him money for his lunch.

For the first time in my life, I got to ride the rides until I had had my fill. But finally even I had had enough of the bumper cars and the roller coaster and the chairs on chains that swung me around like a pail of water.

Aunt Anna took me to a hotdog stand and ordered hotdogs and sodas. Then we found the *Fiaker* and started for the Vienna Woods. When the horses' hooves started to go "clup, clup, clup" again and I told my aunt how much I liked the sound, she didn't reply. She was fast asleep.

She didn't wake up until we arrived, after an hour's ride, at the Vienna Woods next to a large restaurant. We took an outdoor table, and my aunt ordered a light dinner, with a glass of wine for her and one for me.

"You wore me out, Emmy," she said. "I need a glass of wine. Maybe two or three."

From the table, we could see Vienna laid

out before us. Church steeples glistened in the evening sun like pieces of jewelry, St. Stephen's the tallest and most beautiful of all. We could even see the Danube and the Ferris wheel in the Prater.

I was too tired to eat much, but Aunt Anna for once didn't tell me the usual sad story of starving children in India who would be happy to eat what I was wasting. She just asked me if I thought it was getting to be time to go home.

I must have been more tired than I thought, because I went to sleep even before we were out of the Vienna Woods.

Chapter 2

For as long as I could remember, I had liked to "dance." I knew nothing whatever about dancing, of course, and it would be far more accurate to say that all I really did was move my body and my arms and legs around in time with music. But I fondly believed the movements I made were at least as graceful as those of the dancers of the Corps de Ballet I'd seen at the Opera, and probably somewhat more inventive.

I danced for my own pleasure, because I liked it, rather than for the approval of anyone else. Sometimes I danced when my father played waltzes on our electrified Victrola, but he generally preferred what I thought of as "Onkel Otto's music" — that is, opera and symphonic — to something I could dance to, and I was forbidden to operate the Victrola myself.

When my mother was in a good mood, she played our upright piano, invariably with the announcement that she wasn't very good because she didn't practice often enough. Sometimes, my mother played something I could dance to, but she generally preferred music that wasn't right for dancing.

My parents indulged me, but with the exception of my "performances" in the apartment courtyard when the organ grinder came, they were my only audience.

The organ grinder, who came to the inner courtyard of the apartment building about once a month, however, played nothing but music suitable for my dancing. He cranked out one Strauss waltz after another from his wheezing organ, which was mounted on sort of a pushcart. I was somewhat smugly convinced that I was helping the poor man and his little dog earn their living.

Beggars and street musicians are a Viennese tradition at least as old as St. Stephen's Cathedral. Just about every apartment had a *Bettlerschachtel* (beggar's box) by the door. Adults habitually emptied their pockets of small coins, dropping them into the beggar's box as they entered the apartment. When beggars appeared at the door, they were obliged with coins from the box.

Street musicians (usually violinists) who gave their performances in the courtyard also got their pay from the beggar's box. Coins were wrapped in pieces of newspaper and thrown down from the windows.

The organ grinder who regularly came to our courtyard was an old man not really pleasant to look at. His clothes were ragged, badly fitting, and quite dirty. He had a small mongrel dog who rode on top of the organ when his master pushed it. As soon as the organ grinder began to crank the wheel and a Strauss waltz began to wheeze from the organ, the little dog jumped off the pushcart and began to dance on his hind legs.

As soon as I heard the organ begin to play, I raced down the stairs to the courtyard, with Petja, my fox terrier, barking at my heels.

One afternoon several months after my confirmation, the organ grinder appeared in the courtyard. His dog was already dancing when Petja and I raced down to the courtyard. His master gave me a toothless grin, and I started to dance. Petja, baffled by what I was doing, cocked his head and started to bark at me.

The children who had followed the organ grinder and his dog from Mariahilferstrasse into the courtyard watched my dancing in confusion, not sure if I was a regular part of the act, or just crazy.

They didn't mock me, but it wouldn't have bothered me if they had. Not only was I doing what I really loved to do, but at the same time I was helping out the poor organ grinder.

Eventually, far too soon for me, the organ grinder stopped cranking his wheel and looked up expectantly to the windows looking down on the courtyard. The organ grinder's dog, panting, jumped back on the organ box.

In a moment, coins from the beggar's boxes, tightly wrapped in pieces of newspaper, came flying down into the courtyard. Coins from the first and second floors usually stayed wrapped after hitting the cobblestones. Coins from the third, fourth, and fifth floors frequently lost their wrappers in midair, scattering the coins all over.

When all the coins had landed, the organ grinder made a little bow. Then he began to pick up the coins and stuff them into his baggy pants. He was crippled and the children always laughed at him when he awkwardly scurried after the coins. He never missed finding one, however, even when they landed in the bushes. I knew because I always checked after he was gone.

Today, for the first time, the children had laughed at me, and I was embarrassed. I told myself that they had laughed only because Petja had barked at me. They had never laughed before.

But maybe, I thought, I was getting a little old to dance to the organ grinder's music. I had, after all, been confirmed. Maybe they *were* laughing at me.

I went back into the apartment building and started up the stairs even before the organ grinder had rolled his cart from the courtyard, and without checking to see if he had missed any coins.

When I got to my landing, Frau Fischer, the dignified, white-haired old lady who lived on the third floor, was waiting for me. She put out her hand to stop me from going into my apartment.

"I liked your dancing, Emmy," Frau Fischer said. This was a high compliment indeed, for my mother had told me that Frau Fischer had been a mezzo soprano of the Vienna Opera as a younger woman.

"That was the last time I'm ever going to do that," I said.

"Because the children laughed?" she asked.

"No," I said, not wanting to admit that. "Because I am too old."

Frau Fischer laughed. "You're just about old *enough*."

"The kids embarrassed me," I confessed.

"Fools laugh when they are jealous," Frau Fischer said. Then, "Is your mother home?" I nodded, wondering what she wanted with my mother. "Tell her, please, that I would like to speak to her," she went on.

My mother was visibly surprised to see Frau Fischer at our door.

"*Grüss Gott*, Frau Fischer," she said, using the Viennese equivalent of hello.

"Frau Macalik," Frau Fischer asked, "would it be all right if Emmy came to visit me once in a while?"

"Why, of course, Frau Fischer," my mother said, surprised and flattered that a singer of Frau Fischer's reputation would be interested in me. In Vienna, anyone associated with the State Opera is held in near awe. My Uncle Otto, the most prestigious member of the family, was always introduced as "Herr Schober of the Philharmonic."

"May she come tomorrow at three for tea?"

"Yes," my mother said. "Of course, she can."

Later, I asked my mother why Frau Fischer said "for tea" instead of "for coffee." My mother told me that Frau Fischer had traveled a great deal all over the world and had probably acquired a number of strange tastes.

At three o'clock the next day I took the stairs two at a time to the third floor, and pushed the button beside Frau Fischer's polished brass nameplate.

The door was opened by a smiling elderly woman. She wore a black dress with white lace around the collar and wrists, and a short, white, lace-trimmed apron. A wide, stiff band of lace stood up in her gray hair like a crown.

"You must be Emmy," she said. "Please come in." I was surprised that the maid knew my name.

Inside the apartment, she led me to a double door, opened it, and motioned for me to go through. The windows of the room were covered by dark red velvet curtains. A large crystal chandelier hung from the ceiling and four candelabra were on the walls. I thought that if I had a chandelier and candelabra like those I wouldn't open my curtains, either.

"Frau Fischer will be in shortly," the maid said, and then left, closing the door behind her.

I had a chance to look around the room. Except for several velvet-cushioned chairs and a small, white marble-topped table, the only furniture in the room was a grand piano. On it a large crystal vase was filled with freshly cut flowers. There was a large gold-framed photograph of a very pretty, but sad-faced young woman on the small table.

Frau Fischer came into the room.

"*Küss die Hand*," I said. Viennese custom calls for children and young people to say "I kiss your hand" to older women and men, something passed on from the time when people actually kissed the hands of their betters.

"I'm so glad you could come, Emmy," Frau Fischer said. She pointed to one of the chairs next to the small table. "Please sit down."

The maid came in a moment later, carrying a silver tea set on a tray and a folding table to support it. She was introduced to me as Gertrude.

"This is English tea," Frau Fischer said. "We Viennese just don't know anything about good tea." I said nothing. "Will you take lemon or milk, Emmy? And sugar?"

"Two lumps, please," I said. "And lemon."

I was terrified holding the dainty, thin china cup in my hands. Fragile, beautiful things had a way of breaking in my hands.

When I joined my mother and her friends at afternoon coffee, I was always provided with a sturdy mug.

The tea was horrible! I felt like spitting it out. And the English cookies seemed stale.

"I've been watching you dance since you were a tiny girl," Frau Fischer said. "You really love it, don't you?"

"Oh, yes," I said.

Frau Fischer pointed to the framed photograph of the sad-faced young woman on the table.

"My daughter loved to dance, too," she said. "She was a ballerina."

"At the Opera?" I asked.

Frau Fischer nodded. "You remind me of her," she said. "You even have blond hair and blue eyes like hers."

"Where does she live?" I asked.

"I'm afraid she's no longer with us," Frau Fischer said.

"You mean she's dead?" I blurted. Frau Fischer stiffened a moment and then nodded. "What happened to her?" I plunged on.

Frau Fischer didn't reply immediately, giving me time to consider my bad manners. I was frequently in trouble for asking questions that should not be asked, and I had obviously just done it again.

"When she was twenty-three," Frau Fischer finally said, "she decided she didn't want to live anymore."

"Why?" I asked.

"She was in love," Frau Fischer said.

"And that made her not want to live anymore?"

"You really ask a lot of questions, don't you?" Frau Fischer replied.

"I'm sorry," I said.

"The man she was in love with was married," Frau Fischer said. "When she found that out, she committed suicide."

I didn't know what "committing suicide" meant and Frau Fischer, sensing this, went on:

"She shot and killed herself with a pistol," Frau Fischer said. And then, half crying, added: "Right in front of the man."

I told Frau Fischer that was the saddest story I had ever heard in my whole life, and that I was very sorry for her dead daughter.

"I can't imagine what got into me, telling you that story," Frau Fischer said. "Please forgive me."

"It's all right," I replied, graciously.

"But you're so very much like she was," Frau Fischer said, and for a moment I thought she was going to start crying again. But then she stood up, smiled very brightly, and asked, "If I sing for you, will you then dance for me?"

Without waiting for an answer she went to the piano. She carefully removed the crystal vase and fresh flowers, and then propped the top of the piano open.

In a light, gentle voice, Frau Fischer sang of pretty flowers, Viennese girls, and people in love. I thought she sounded even better than the singers at the Opera, and the way she played the piano made my mother and Olaf Jensen sound as if they had just begun to take lessons. I thought I could listen to Frau Fischer play and sing forever.

After perhaps thirty minutes, she stopped. "And now, please, you will dance for me?" she asked.

I walked toward the center of the room and waited for her to begin playing.

"No, no!" Frau Fischer said, throwing her arms up. "You can't dance in those shoes. Take them off." I couldn't believe what I was hearing. "And your socks, too. Otherwise, you will slip."

I would never have thought that any adult would let me take off my shoes and socks, much less insist on it. I remembered what my mother had said about Frau Fischer learning strange customs in foreign places. I sat down and took off my shoes and socks.

When I was barefoot, Frau Fischer began to play a slow Strauss waltz, and I began to dance. I moved my arms slowly downward and then way up over my head, meanwhile moving in what I was sure were graceful circles. Frau Fischer applauded when I had finished, then began to play what I recognized (because my friend Olaf played them) to be Chopin waltzes.

As Frau Fischer played, more beautifully, I realized, than even the pianists on my father's gramophone records, I danced —

I have no idea for how long — oblivious to everything but the music. But eventually Frau Fischer stopped playing, said that that was enough and that I should put my shoes and socks on.

"I liked the way you danced, Emmy," she said. "You danced with the music. In ballet, it is so important to have an ear for music." I smiled with pleasure. I had done something right.

"How old are you, Emmy?" Frau Fischer asked.

"I'm eight," I answered.

"Just the right age," Frau Fischer said. "How would you like to go to school and learn to really dance?"

"I'd love it!" I said instantly.

"You would have to work every day, and very hard," she cautioned.

"Dancing isn't work," I said.

"You'll quickly find out that it is," Frau Fischer said. She glanced at the photograph of her daughter. "I'll have a talk with your mother," she said, as if she had made up her mind.

The moment I got home, I told my mother how absolutely wonderful Frau Fischer was: "She played the piano, Straus and Chopin! She even sang! And she *asked* me to dance for her, and said she liked it; and her daughter shot herself with a pistol; and Frau Fischer is going to send me to school so I can learn how to really dance."

From the look on my mother's face, I concluded she hadn't believed a word I said. She certainly didn't seem very interested.

For several weeks I heard nothing of going to dancing school, but then when I walked into Frau Fischer's apartment for one of the regular Tuesday teas, she had an announcement for me:

"Some old friends are coming to tea today, Emmy," she said, "and I want you to dance for them."

Before I had time to think this over, the doorbell rang and there were male voices in the entrance hall. Gertrude showed three elderly gentlemen into the music room. They all had snow-white hair and wore black suits, brightly colored ties, vests with gold watch chains, and shiny black shoes. One was tall and skinny with a long nose; one was medium-sized, and one was short. The short one wore a monocle. Ordinarily, three elderly men would have frightened me, or at least made me uneasy. But for some reason, this trio did not alarm me.

They each bowed and kissed Frau Fischer's hand.

"And this is my young friend, Emmy," she said, putting her hand on my shoulder.

I said *"Küss die Hand"* and made my curtsy. The old men smiled, but didn't seem particularly interested in me.

Frau Fischer sat me down between herself and the short man. Then she made the ritual announcement: "Gertrude is going to bring us tea and cookies."

And Gertrude did. The tea was as horrible and the cookies as stale as ever. I wondered if the old men really liked them, or were just pretending as I was.

They talked about someone they knew who had just gotten married and returned from the wedding trip. For some reason they thought this was funny. After a while, the tall one touched Frau Fischer's hand and asked her to sing.

The top of the piano was already up. I realized that Frau Fischer had known that she would be asked to play. While she sang, the three old gentlemen looked at her as if they were sitting in a theater and she was the star, and when she finished, they applauded quietly.

"Now we have a special treat," Frau Fischer said. She winked at me.

I quickly took my shoes and socks off, went to the center of the room, and waited for Frau Fischer to begin playing. I was more than a little uncomfortable, but when the music began my legs began to tingle and the world around me disappeared.

When Frau Fischer stopped playing, the three old gentlemen applauded. I made a little curtsy. The medium-sized man patted me on the top of my head when I said good-bye, and said he would look forward to seeing me again.

This was the first time anybody I didn't know had applauded my dancing, and I was delighted.

Chapter 3

Over the next couple of months, my Tuesday visits to Frau Fischer became something of a ritual. I appeared, tea was served, she sang, and I danced. Her three gentlemen friends appeared from time to time, but most often it was just Frau Fischer and me. My mother told my father that it was "nice that Emmy can give Frau Fischer some company." And obviously, it got me out from under her feet in a situation where I wouldn't get into trouble.

The first thing out of the ordinary occurred one afternoon when I came home from Frau Fischer's apartment and found my mother suddenly all excited about the world of music.

"You won't believe who I saw in the foyer," she said, in awe: "Maestro *Richard Strauss*!"

"Oh," I replied, wholly unimpressed, "he usually brings me a little piece of *Sachertorte* from Demel's."

"*Maestro Richard Strauss*," my mother

asked incredulously, "brings *you Sachertorte?*"

"Sometimes *Sachertorte,* sometimes just
cookies," I explained. "He's an old friend of
Frau Fischer. He comes to watch me dance."

"But you don't really know who he is, do
you?" my mother asked. I didn't know what
she meant. She put a record on the Victrola.
(I recognized the music, a waltz, but I didn't
know the name and said as much.)

"Do you know what that is?" she asked,
and went on without waiting for a reply.
"That's from *Der Rosenkavalier,* by *Richard
Strauss.*"

"I knew he had something to do with the
Opera," I said smugly.

Two days after that, without any sort of
preliminaries, Frau Fischer appeared at our
door, refused my mother's offer of coffee,
and announced that she wanted to talk to her
about putting me "into the ballet school at
the Opera."

My mother was flabbergasted. The best she
could manage was the announcement that
"Emmy hasn't had any training whatso-
ever."

"She has a natural talent," Frau Fischer
replied.

"She's only eight," my mother persisted.

"That's exactly the right age," Frau
Fischer countered. "They like to start training them when they're about eight, when
their bodies are still malleable."

"Well, I'm grateful to you, Frau Fischer,"

my mother said finally. "I never even thought about anything like this."

"I'd like your permission to go ahead," Frau Fischer said. "To get in touch with the right people at the Opera."

"Yes, of course," my mother said.

Frau Fischer shook hands with my mother, smiled at me, patted me on my head, and left.

My mother met my father at the door with the news. I had been sent to my room when he was about to arrive home, but sensing something about me was to be discussed, I had left the door open a crack to eavesdrop.

"Well, it sounds fine to me," my father said. "If Emmy wants to go, let her. It won't cost us a *Schilling*. The ballet school is like the Vienna Boys Choir. The State pays for it. It would be better for her than running around with Marcella and her brother all the time."

A week later Frau Fischer handed my mother a sheet of paper. "The audition is only once a year and we just made it," she said. "I've everything written down. The date, time, and where to go."

"My husband and I are grateful to you for all your trouble," my mother said.

"Emmy's something special," Frau Fischer said. I was eavesdropping again, and I was thrilled. No one had ever said anything like that about me before.

On the day of the audition, I put on my confirmation dress.

"And where are you going all dressed up, so early in the morning?" my father teased when he saw me.

"You know very well where I'm going."

"I want to talk to you about it," he said seriously, motioning for me to sit down at the breakfast table with him.

"Don't go there with the idea that you're sure to win," he began. "Sometimes in life things don't go the way we would like them to go. And it could easily happen that they won't want you. But, if things go the wrong way, I'll see what I can do about sending you to another ballet school."

In the streetcar on the way to the Opera, I thought that over. I decided that if I didn't get accepted, that was it. I would give up dancing. It was either the Staatsoper ballet school or nothing!

When we got to the Opera House, an enormous stone building that occupies a full block on the Ring at the corner of Kärntnerstrasse, we saw a crowd of girls and their mothers moving toward a huge door on the left of the building. Most of the girls were about my age, but some of them were older. They were obviously going to the audition, too. There was one lonely boy among them.

Inside the Opera House, the ceiling was as high as that of my church and there was even a churchlike echo. People whispered. On the second floor, however, there was a noise like a flock of geese echoing through the halls. As my mother and I followed the crowd through a huge hall, the chattering noise grew louder until we reached the dressing room. There I saw that the gabbling geese were half a hundred girls changing into ballet costumes at long rows of wooden benches and clothing racks running down the center of the dressing room.

I had never seen ballet shoes up close and watched in fascination as one of the girls put hers on. From the swift, sure way she tied the ankle straps, I could tell she had been doing it a long time.

"Frau Fischer must have been mistaken telling us not to bring any ballet clothes and shoes," I whispered to my mother.

"You don't have ballet shoes or clothes," she replied. "Besides, there are other girls in street clothes."

That was true. But there *were* girls in short ballet skirts, tutus, who looked like ballet dancers, and I wondered what chance I would have competing against them. My pretty confirmation dress had suddenly become absolutely the wrong thing to be wearing. I felt like crying.

A woman's voice called out: "The ones who are ready, please, stand in line!"

A line quickly formed. My mother and I went to the end of it. In the line ahead of me stood a dark-haired girl about my age wearing a pink tutu and pink ballet shoes. She turned around and looked down her nose at me in my confirmation dress.

I stuck my tongue out at her. Righteousness outraged, the girl quickly turned and hissed a report of the insult into her mother's ear. The mother turned to give me a dirty look. I smiled innocently back at her.

There were too many people ahead of us in line for me to see what was going on, and when I turned around there were even more people behind us. Then someone gave my mother a piece of cardboard with the number twenty-seven printed on it.

Almost immediately, the woman who had ordered us to form in line called out, "Numbers One to Thirty, please, follow me!"

My mother smiled encouragingly at me and put her arm around my shoulders. We marched with the other girls and their mothers into a room at the end of the hall. The room, as large as the gymnasium of my school, had a smooth, dull, wooden floor. Three of the walls were covered with mirrors; the fourth had windows. Wooden hand railings were fastened to the mirrored walls. An elderly man sat before a grand piano in one corner of the room.

Except for the piano near the window, the only furniture in the room was a large, overstuffed leather sofa and two matching chairs. A group of about ten people, obviously connected with the audition, stood around talking. They were too far away for me to hear what they were saying.

A loud, no-nonsense female voice ordered everyone to move against the mirrored walls. I was surprised to see that such an authoritarian voice had come from such a pretty young woman.

"Number One!" she bellowed. "Please come forward with your mother!"

"Forward," I decided, must be where the young woman stood in front of the group of people. A girl wearing a complete ballet outfit left the front of the line, holding tightly onto her mother's hand. The young woman said something to them, and then the girl walked alone to the center of the room.

One of the men in the group signaled to the old man at the piano, who began to play a Strauss waltz. The girl began to dance. After a few moments I immodestly decided that I was a better dancer than the girl in the ballet outfit was.

After no more than three minutes, the music stopped. The girl returned to her mother, and they walked out of the room.

"Number Two, please!" the pretty young woman called out.

Girl Number Two wore a street dress and was barefoot. I was happy to see that; I wouldn't be the only one barefoot and in a regular dress.

I noticed a boy waiting with his mother by the entrance door, and wondered how well he would do.

My mother touched my elbow to get my attention, and then nodded approvingly toward the girl who was dancing. I smiled politely, but I didn't think much of the girl's dancing. In my judgment, she didn't quite move in time with the beat of the music, and she kept her arms rigid, and in the same stiff and awkward position.

As the numbers called out came closer and closer to mine, I realized that the old man had been playing only Strauss waltzes. That worried me. I danced, I was firmly convinced, much better to Chopin than to Strauss.

"Mama!" the girl in front of us, the one whose superior look had let me know what she thought of my confirmation dress, suddenly wailed, "I don't want to go out there!"

"Don't be silly," her mother replied, firmly and coldly. "Of course you do."

"I *won't*!" she sobbed. "And you can't make me!"

Her mother pinched the skin of the girl's upper arm and twisted it. I knew that it must have been very painful. I couldn't understand why the girl didn't scream — I certainly would have — but the girl didn't make a sound.

Number Twenty-six was called out. The girl's mother, her hand still pinching her daughter's arm, propelled her across the room.

When the girl, after an awkward first few moments, began to dance, I saw that she was much more graceful than I was, and that she could make movements I didn't know how to make. I hoped for the girl's sake that she would be accepted; it was obvious that her mother would be furious with her if she wasn't.

And then, all of a sudden, while standing on her toes, the girl lost her balance and fell flat on her behind.

The old man continued to play, and the woman in charge seemed to expect the girl to get up and continue, but when she got up, she ran, crying, to her mother. I felt really sorry for her.

I didn't hear my number being called, but my mother did, and led me by the hand to the group of people at the leather sofa. At last, I thought, I would find out what they were talking about. A man asked me for my name; another asked what music I would like.

"A Chopin waltz, please," I answered, half afraid that the old man could play only Strauss waltzes.

"Chopin waltz!" the man called out loudly. He hadn't seemed surprised, and as I took off my shoes and socks, I was enormously relieved.

I went to the center of the room and waited for the music to begin. The moment I heard the familiar lilting Chopin, my legs began to tingle. I started to dance. As soon as I began to move, to turn, I realized I could dance in much larger circles here than I had been able to do in Frau Fischer's music room.

And I thought that for however long it lasted, this enormous room was mine, and with it the biggest audience I had ever had. I loved it!

When the music stopped, I was disappointed. I returned to my mother and put my socks and shoes back on. One of the women who had been watching, and who was, I thought, as pretty as a movie star, came over to us.

"Where does your daughter go to school?" she asked.

"She goes to Saint Mary's," my mother replied.

"What *ballet* school?" the woman pursued.

"She doesn't go to ballet school," my mother said. "And never has."

"Frau Macalik," the attractive woman said, patiently, "everybody tells us that. How long has she been studying?"

"She hasn't had any training of any kind," my mother said firmly. I knew that tone of voice.

Another attractive woman came over.

"This is Emmy Macalik," she said. "The girl Frau Fischer told us about." When that didn't register, she added, "Don't you remember? Otto Schober's niece? But we won't hold that against her." Then they both laughed.

I knew what would happen next. My mother didn't like Uncle Otto, but she would not stand for anyone else criticizing him, and that would be the end of Emmy Macalik and ballet school.

But before my mother could open her

mouth, the young woman handed her an envelope.

"Would you fill out these forms and return them as quickly as you can?" she asked. My mother for once was speechless. "You'll be hearing from us in a week or so," the young woman said, and walked away.

I was glad that the audition was finally over. I didn't want to think about whether or not I had been accepted.

My mother took me to a coffeehouse around the corner from the Opera for sandwiches and lemonade, and then we went home.

Three weeks later the mailman brought an envelope with The Vienna State Opera printed on it. It was addressed to my mother, but I couldn't wait for her. I ripped it open and read that I had been accepted.

I ran to our apartment and showed the letter to my mother. Then I snatched the letter from her hand and ran up the stairs to show it to Frau Fischer. When Gertrude answered my ring, she didn't smile at me as she usually did.

"May I please see Frau Fischer?" I asked. "I have something to show her."

"Not today, Emmy," Gertrude said. "I'm afraid Frau Fischer is not well." She smiled at me and closed the door.

I felt like crying. There was nobody in the whole world whom I wanted more to tell I had been accepted than Frau Fischer. My mother was pleased, and my father would be happy for me when he found out, but neither of them would be as happy as Frau Fischer would. Frau Fischer *understood* what it was with me and dancing.

Day after day I climbed the stairs after school to ask Gertrude if Frau Fischer was well enough to see me, but the answer was always the same: "Frau Fischer is not doing very well today, Emmy. Perhaps tomorrow."

Two weeks later when I started up the stairs, my mother stopped me and told me that Frau Fischer had been taken to the hospital.

"Can I go see her there?"

"I'm sorry, Emmy," my mother said. "I asked. She's too sick to have visitors."

Every night before I went to sleep I prayed, and prayed, and prayed for Frau Fischer to get well.

My prayers went unheeded. When I came home from school one afternoon, my mother told me that Frau Fischer had "died peacefully" in her sleep. I didn't know how somebody could die "peacefully," but I understood that Frau Fischer, my friend, was dead.

Her funeral was held two days later. My mother wore a dark blue suit with a hat, gloves, and shoes to match. I wore my school uniform because there had not been enough time to go home and change.

The funeral home was near Vienna's huge

municipal cemetery, the Zentralfriedhof. Among the more than fifty people standing around inside, I recognized Gertrude and Herr Strauss and his two friends. Gertrude wore black. When she saw me and smiled at me, I saw that her eyes were swollen and red. Neither Maestro Strauss nor his two friends seemed to notice me.

My mother and Gertrude spoke in whispers. I didn't want to talk to anybody. I walked across the room to the casket, which was almost hidden behind a bank of flowers. Their smell reminded me of the flowers in St. Stephen's. When I first saw the casket, I was momentarily frightened, but it was closed and after a moment I was all right. But when I thought about Frau Fischer and how kind she had been to me, and that I would never see her anymore, tears ran down my cheeks.

I felt a hand on my shoulder, and, thinking it was my mother, I turned around to throw my arms around her. But it wasn't my mother. It was Maestro Strauss. I was embarrassed and disengaged myself from him.

"She wouldn't want you, Emmy, of all people, to cry," Maestro Strauss said. He took out his handkerchief and wiped my tears and made me blow my nose. "I think she would want you to say a prayer for her," he said. "She loved you. And you must think that now she is in heaven with her daughter. That's what she's wanted for some time."

I started to cry again, much louder now

than before, and threw my arms around the old man and hid my face in his vest. I didn't care if it was polite or not. I didn't care about anything anymore. It was the first time in my whole life that someone I loved had died. It was an unbearable feeling of loneliness.

Maestro Strauss finally, gently, pried me loose, wiped my tears again, and told me that he had to join his friends. My mother took my hand and led me to another room. It was something like the Mariahilferkirche, our parish church. Not nearly as large, or as old, but there were stained-glass windows and in the front of the room, huge white candles flickered in front of a four-foot golden cross mounted on the wall. Gertrude came in and sat across the aisle from us.

A moment later, the casket was carried into the room by Maestro Strauss, his two friends, and one other man. Everyone stood up as the casket was carried in. It looked to me as if the four old gentlemen were having trouble carrying it.

An elderly monsignor walked behind the casket, and a curate followed him. Both wore black robes. The monsignor's robe was ornately stitched and the white surplice he wore over it was made entirely of lace. The curate's cassock and surplice had no designs or lace.

Frau Fischer's friends gently lowered her casket onto supports between the candles, then sat down in the first pew. The monsignor went to the tall wooden stand and began to talk about Frau Fischer. He reminded the small group of her mourners what a great and gentle lady she had been, how her singing, in opera and in concert all over the world, had made so many people happy. Finally, he finished, crossed himself, turned toward the cross, went on his knees, and began to pray in Latin. Everyone joined in The Lord's Prayer. Maestro Strauss and his three friends then picked up the casket and slowly carried it out of the room.

The cemetery was a block away. Maestro Strauss, his three friends, Gertrude, and my mother and I walked immediately behind the hearse, the other mourners behind us. The hearse was an oblong glass box on a carriage drawn by four black horses. Tall, narrow black vases holding tall black feathers hung from each corner. Black curtains inside were drawn open, and the casket inside could be seen. The coachman's suit and gloves were black, and he wore a tall black feather on his top hat. Even the horses had black feathers on the sides of their heads.

As far as I was concerned, they should have decorated the hearse with the brightest flowers they could find. Frau Fischer had loved bright flowers. The huge crystal vase on top of her piano had always been full of them. I wondered what had happened to the bright flowers at the funeral home.

In the cemetery, I found out: They had been arranged around a big oblong hole in the ground to hide the raw earth.

Maestro Strauss and the other men carried Frau Fischer's casket from the hearse to the hole, and onto the straps of a machine, which would lower it into the grave.

Then Maestro Strauss came to me and put his hand on my shoulder. His three friends stood behind us.

The monsignor went to the side of the casket, and intoned, *"Dominus vobiscum."* Everyone answered with *"Et cum spiritu tuo."* He sprinkled Holy Water from a silver vessel onto the casket, and the casket began to sink slowly into the grave.

The curate picked up a small gray metal bucket in both hands. He held it out to the monsignor, who reached into it and took out a small trowel filled with dirt. The monsignor made the Sign of the Cross and shook dirt from the trowel into the grave. One of Frau Fischer's old friends took the trowel from him and did exactly the same thing. One by one the others followed suit. The monsignor folded his hands, closed his eyes, and prayed silently.

My mother pushed me up to the curate. I took a trowel full of dirt and stepped to the edge of the grave. I could see Frau Fischer's casket with the dirt splattered on it. I hated to think that Frau Fischer was *really* down there and that I was going to have to throw dirt on her. But I tipped the trowel up and dirt spilled from it into the grave.

I was supposed to make the Sign of the Cross, but as if with a mind of my own, my knees bent and I did my last curtsy to my friend.

Then I threw the trowel to the ground, turned around to my mother, and threw myself into her arms.

Chapter 4

It was fall, and the leaves had started to fall from the chestnut trees along the Ring, but the day was sunny and warm when my mother led me up the side staircase of the Opera to the second floor rehearsal hall for my first day at ballet school. I was dressed for the occasion in a red and blue pleated skirt, a jacket to match, a white blouse with a red and blue plaid bow, white knee-length stockings, and new blue shoes.

The letter from the Opera had ordered my mother to bring me to the rehearsal hall no later than three o'clock on Monday afternoon. Frau Fischer had been buried the previous Friday.

When we reached the dressing room, about twenty girls were already there. Half were wearing white-trimmed navy blue ballet tights and ballet slippers.

From their self-confidence, I could tell that they were not nervous newcomers.

A girl in tights was stationed by the

dressing room entrance to politely tell the mothers that they couldn't stay with their daughters, and that they should come back for them at five. I was frankly relieved when she told my mother she had to leave. I didn't want her hovering protectively over me all afternoon.

A girl introduced herself to me as Sissy Gruber. Sissy had been a common Viennese nickname ever since it got out that Empress Elizabeth was called Sissy. Sissy Gruber asked my name, and then said she was going to help me get started.

She led me to a rack and handed me a set of tights. "Try this one on for size," she said, "while I get you some slippers."

I had just finished pulling on the stretch-knit cotton tights when someone tapped my shoulder. I turned around and saw the girl who had fallen on her backside at the audition. I saw, too, that the tights she was wearing were too large for her. The girl had apparently forgotten that I had stuck my tongue out at her, or at least had forgiven me, for she was smiling.

"I'm glad you're here," she said. "I don't feel so alone."

"I'm glad to see you, too," I admitted.

"I'm Ilse," the girl said. "Who are you?" I told her. We shook hands.

Sissy returned with three pairs of white cotton ballet slippers, none of which fit when I tried them on. She went to get more.

When I finally had a pair I could get my

feet in, Sissy showed me how to tie them: First, a thin, round cord around the opening of the slipper had to be drawn tight and tied in a bow. The bow was then pushed inside the slipper over the toes.

Each slipper had two ribbons, about a foot long and three quarters of an inch wide, attached near the heel. First, they were crossed in front of the ankle, then in back, then again in front, and finally, they were tied in a knot — not a bow — against the rear ankle. The loose ends of the knot were then laced in and around the strap.

"In my ballet school we tied the knot at the side of our ankles," Ilse, who had been watching, announced, smugly professional.

"I'm not surprised," Sissy replied, even more smugly. "Some schools even tie the knot in a bow that hangs down in the front of the ankle. A bow or a strap hanging down breaks the graceful line of your ankle."

Ilse was not ready to give up. She picked up my other slipper and pushed on the toe.

"The toes are soft!" she said disdainfully. "I've been wearing toe shoes for two years."

"Don't let Frau Dertl hear you say that," Sissy said. "If you want my advice, don't say another word about anything you've done before."

Ilse thought it over, and then I could see by her face that she had resigned herself to be as much of a rookie as I was. Sissy must have seen surrender, too, for she explained: "You'll wear soft slippers here until your muscles are trained and your bones won't be harmed by standing on your toes."

We were taken to the large, mirror-walled rehearsal room where the auditions had been held.

The woman who had talked to me and my mother at the audition was standing in the center of the room. She wore street clothes, a blouse and a billowing skirt, but her feet were strapped into black ballet slippers.

"I am Frau Dertl," the woman announced. "I will be your teacher. The girls who have been helping you are my better students," she said. "They will be your guides for a while, until you understand what is expected of you. If you have a question, ask them." Sissy smiled at me; she was apparently to be my personal guide.

"Congratulations!" Frau Dertl said, very formally and very seriously. "You are now *élèves*, students of the classical ballet. *Élèves* of the Wiener Staatsoper Ballet!"

I was thrilled. Frau Dertl's announcement made my dream official.

Then Frau Dertl got right down to business.

"Some of you have had some 'training' in private schools," she began. "Forget everything you may think you have learned. The Vienna State Opera Corps de Ballet has its own rules. Obey them or leave the ballet. Some of you may even own, or actually have been wearing, *pointe* [toe] slippers. If so, throw them away! By the time you will be

51

permitted to wear them here, you will have outgrown them. Anyone I see wearing them will be sent home.

"No one here is going to tell you how cute you look in your fancy tutu, standing on your toes! Beginners don't wear tutus or *pointe* slippers. That will come after you have learned the discipline and the skills necessary for classical ballet.

"You will be here and ready every day at three o'clock. If you are late or don't feel like showing up at all, don't bother. We won't miss you. But don't come back!

"There were over three hundred applicants at the audition. We selected forty who might have talent. By the end of the year, half of you will either have dropped out or have been sent home.

"It will be up to you to make something of the opportunity we offer. In other words, if you stick by our rules, we can help you to become classical dancers. If you don't stick to our rules, out you go!"

She went to the piano and picked up what looked like a broomstick. She pointed it at the elderly, gray-haired pianist whom I remembered from the audition.

"This is our dear old friend Herr Schnitzer. He has been with us for many, many years. He has seen many young girls like you become dancers and ballerinas. When I was an *élève*, I cried on Herr Schnitzer's shoulder when I thought my teacher had pushed me too far. He always told me that I should try a little harder. If you're very lucky one day, you might be able to be Herr Schnitzer's friend, too."

She banged her stick twice on the floor, and Herr Schnitzer began to play. Chopin, I realized with delight.

Frau Dertl put her free arm out to the side and, her heels touching, sank slowly, effortlessly, and gracefully toward the floor. Then, just as slowly, effortlessly, and gracefully she rose again.

"This exercise is called the *plié*," she said, starting down again. "*Plié* is a French term. Ballet has many French terms. Even the railing is called by its French name, *barre*."

Now she was coming up again. Her movements were beautiful. Her arm and hand and head moved in perfect coordination with her other movements.

"Pierre Beauchamp, the choreographer of the Paris Opera, developed, two hundred years ago, the set of *barre* exercises every major ballet in the world uses today," she said.

All the time she was talking she was going up and down, with graceful swoops of her arms and with absolutely no apparent effort. I could hardly wait to try it.

"The *barre* positions he invented," she said, "are the basis for classical ballet. They are practiced in exactly the same way by *élèves*, dancers, ballerinas, and principal dancers."

She rose again in one smooth, fluid motion,

but this time she stayed erect. The music stopped.

"The advanced *élèves* will show you how to do the *plié*," she announced.

Sissy showed me how to hold on to the *barre*. I had grabbed it from the bottom. You were supposed to place the hand on top. Then she showed me how my feet were to be placed: heels together and feet forming a straight line.

When I tried it, I could do it, but I couldn't hold the position for more than a few seconds. My feet kept slipping forward, out of line.

Sissy bent down and pushed them back into the prescribed position. I felt an uncomfortable strain on my muscles.

Then I tried to slowly bend my legs while Sissy forced my knees apart.

"That hurts!" I complained.

"Hold on to the *barre*!" Sissy warned.

Too late! I lost my balance and fell backward. I heard laughter. I was being laughed at! But when I looked around, I saw other girls sitting on the floor, too. The laughter wasn't only for me.

"What did I do wrong?" I asked.

"Watch me!" Sissy replied.

Just as effortlessly as Frau Dertl had, Sissy began to sink and rise in the graceful movements of the *plié*, keeping time with the slow waltz from Herr Schnitzer's piano.

"You see?" Sissy asked. I didn't see at all, but I tried it. I got down all right, but when I was halfway back up, I lost my balance again. This time I fell forward. Sissy caught me.

"I knew this was going to happen," she laughed. "You'll get it."

I felt even worse when I saw Ilse. She was by no means graceful, but at least she was going up and down without knocking people over.

"Don't worry," Frau Dertl said softly in my ear. I hadn't heard her come up. "Your muscles are not trained. They will learn quickly. Try it again!"

About the kindest thing that could be said about my third attempt at a *plié* was that I didn't knock anybody else down. And, actually within a couple of minutes, I was soon able to relax my death-grip on the *barre* and get up and down with relative ease, if without very much grace.

Getting up and down at all gave me the self-confidence to try to move my arms in the graceful way Sissy and Frau Dertl moved theirs. Someone touched me on the shoulder. It was Frau Dertl again.

"Don't bother about your arm movements, Emmy," she said. "Just hold your arm straight out. We'll get to arm movements later."

When I did my next *plié*, Sissy, standing behind me, pulled my shoulders straight.

"Keep your back as straight as if you had swallowed a broom," she said. "And never look down. Chin up! Try it again."

I felt less awkward with my back straight, but after a few more *pliés* the muscles in my legs began to tremble. Sissy saw me shaking and saw that I was embarrassed by it.

"Your leg muscles are just not used to this kind of strain," Sissy said. "They'll get used to it. You're doing great for your first day." I didn't believe a word Sissy said.

Finally the music stopped and Frau Dertl said, "I think that's enough for your first day, girls."

It was for me. By then I was tired, sweaty, dizzy, and ready to leave. But there was more. Sissy took me by the hand and we trotted over to Herr Schnitzer at the piano. She seemed to float lightly over the floor. I thought we probably looked like a gazelle leading a water buffalo.

"*Danke schön*, Herr Schnitzer," Sissy called, and squeezed my hand as a signal for me to thank him, too.

"*Danke schön*, Herr Schnitzer," I parroted.

Then Sissy trotted us over to Frau Dertl. She made a curtsy and said "*Küss die Hand*." I now knew what was expected of me, and when I came up from my curtsy Frau Dertl patted me on my head. Finally, Sissy trotted off to the dressing room, dragging me behind her.

"You always greet Frau Dertl and Herr Schnitzer before the lesson," Sissy said, "and thank them afterward."

While I was changing into my street clothes, Sissy got me another set of tights.

"One for wearing and one for washing," she said. "And you'd better get yourself a small carrying case." I nodded my understanding. Sissy smiled at me again. "You did very well for your first day, Emmy," she said. "I'll see you tomorrow."

My mother was waiting with the other mothers just outside the dressing room. She took my hand and led me down the stairs and to the streetcar stop on Ringstrasse. As we waited for the streetcar, I looked back at the Opera House and tried to digest the amazing truth: I *really was* a member of the Vienna State Opera Ballet! I already knew how to do a *plié*.

Chapter 5

I think my mother was impressed, and certainly surprised, by how seriously I took my ballet lessons. In any event, after several weeks I was able to convince her that it would be safe for me to go alone to the Opera for my daily lessons.

By then, I had learned the five *barre* exercises. They ranged from small movements of the feet to complicated exercises involving coordinated movements of the legs and the body itself.

Barre exercises are designed primarily to do two things. First, they develop, and make limber, the bones and muscles of the body. Second, they prepare the student to eventually dance (and dancers and even ballerinas to practice) the steps of classical ballet.

The *battement tendu* didn't look difficult at first. The leg is extended, knee straight, first in front, until the toes brush the floor, and then to the side and rear. The apparent ease with which Sissy demonstrated the *batte-ment tendu* made me think even I could do it. But pointing *my* moving leg outward, and keeping it straight at the same time, proved to be far more difficult than it looked. I had only one foot on the floor to give me balance, and that one foot had to be held in a pre-scribed position, flat on the floor, toes out-ward, and in a line with my shoulders.

Ballet dancers can spot one another in a crowd on a busy street. Only ballet dancers walk with their feet pointed outward in a position learned and made unforgettable at the *barre*.

The *grand battement* exercise is performed with the leg at hip level (instead of barely brushing the floor). My moving leg was sup-posed to go up and down in time with the music. I had great difficulty with the second part. If I made the movements reasonably correctly, I was a beat too late, or if I was in time with the music, my movements quickly drew Frau Dertl's correction.

The *rond de jambe* is actually two different exercises. I didn't find the first one difficult. While my toes lightly brushed the floor I had to move my leg in a half circle from the front, sideward to the rear, and then repeat the exercise by moving my leg from the back sideward to the front.

The second part of the *rond de jambe* is the same movement, but with the leg raised to hip level. When I held my back straight, I could not raise my leg to hip level and move it. It just wouldn't go. I tried until I felt like crying.

If I didn't raise my leg quite to hip level, I could almost move it to the back. But the slow movement required put so much strain on my leg and back that I couldn't keep my leg up as long as I was supposed to.

When Frau Dertl saw that I was really having trouble with the *rond de jambe*, she came to help. She held my leg up as high as it was supposed to be, and supported it while I moved it back and forth in time with the music. I could hear my joints popping as Frau Dertl moved me back and forth.

It was a very long time before I could do the elevated *rond de jambe* without support, and an even longer time before my movements acquired any semblance of grace.

I also had problems with the *développé*, which is the slow straightening of the bent leg at hip level, front, side, and rear. The movement itself is difficult for untrained bodies, and the strain of holding the leg in the extended positions until the music permits it to be slowly lowered approaches agony.

When we students finished our *barre* exercises, we went to the middle of the room to do floor exercises, which are intended to teach balance and coordinated movement, as well as to provide the same kind of muscle flexing the *barre* exercises do. The *barre* and the floor exercises provided practice in movements that would ultimately permit us to dance the *cabriole, entrechat, jeté,* and the other movements of classical ballet.

Although I certainly thought the opposite at the time, we new *élèves* were not really subjected to much of a strain on our bodies for the first few weeks. But after we had learned the basic movements at the *barre* and the floor exercises, and our muscles had begun to adapt to the new strains put to them, the intensity of instruction increased.

It was now presumed that we knew what was expected of us, and it actually got brutal. If I (or any other *élève*) did the exercise wrong, it was because I wasn't trying. And once I had learned to make the movements satisfactorily but wasn't making them in exact time with Herr Schnitzer's piano, it was because I wasn't trying. And if my movements were correct and in time but not especially graceful, it was because I wasn't trying.

There was genuine pain, not only at the *barre* and on the floor, but at home at night. My muscles always ached and often went into painful spasms, the charley horse familiar to athletes.

I asked Sissy: "How long was it before you stopped hurting?"

Sissy was shocked at the question. "Whatever gave you the idea that I don't hurt?"

"Everything you do seems so easy for you, and you never complain about the pain."

"I don't complain because I love the ballet," Sissy said firmly. "But I hurt. Not as much as you, maybe, but I hurt. Every dancer hurts. I got used to the pain and so will you."

The moment Frau Dertl thought we *élèves* had learned the basic leg exercises (but long before we had *mastered* them), she began to teach us the coordinated movements of the head and arms and hands.

"The movement of the upper body, the head, arms, and hands must be as graceful as the movement of the legs," she said. "Basically, the arm and hand follow the movement of the leg, and the head and eyes follow the movement of the hand. The face should show pleasure, a little smile. Not a smirk; ballet isn't funny. Just a pleased look. I don't want to see anyone's teeth."

Frau Dertl had as much trouble getting the "proper look" on the faces of a roomful of little girls as she did teaching us the movements. We were either grimacing with pain, or studies in grim determination, or, rarely, in giggles. The dignified smiles of pleasure Frau Dertl wanted were a long time in coming.

For some reason, I must have appeared sad when I was concentrating, for one of my most clear memories is of Frau Dertl asking me, with mock compassion in her voice, who had died.

I remember, too, Frau Dertl's speech about the fingers: "Keep your fingers straight but not as stiff as a soldier saluting. Don't let your thumbs hang down! Hold them nearly even with your fingers. A dancer's hands are the most eloquent part of her body. You may have noticed that I never hit you on the hands. The back and legs, naturally, but never the hands."

When Frau Dertl ran out of parts of the body that could be moved, she came up with something else:

One day, a month or so later, while we *élèves* were doing an easy exercise, with Frau Dertl keeping time by banging her stick on the floor and calling out, "One, two, and a three! One, two, and a three!" she suddenly stopped.

"Some of you don't listen to the music," she shouted angrily. "And those who do listen obviously don't understand it! I won't have this! A dancer must know music!" She waited until this had sunk in, and then went on:

"Your next assignment is to study a musical instrument. I don't expect you to become a pianist or violinist, but two years of musical training should give you some understanding. Talk it over at home, and when I next meet with your mothers, they can tell me what arrangements you have made."

In the dressing room I asked Sissy what instrument she studied.

"I took piano for two years," she told me. "I actually got to like it."

"I'll take piano, too," I instantly decided. I had fooled around with our piano. It seemed a much easier instrument to play than Uncle Otto's violin. And unless I handled my mother right and got started right away on the piano, I was liable to find myself being taught to play the violin by Uncle Otto.

Whenever I see, all too rarely, a girl from those days, we invariably recall being beaten by Frau Dertl's stick. I have told the same stories, but in truth, we're really being unfair to Frau Dertl. She never really *beat* anyone, although she had frequently used her stick. We *élèves* got it on the leg when our leg was not straight or high enough; on the back when the back wasn't straight; on the ankle when the feet weren't in the correct position. Frau Dertl hit just hard enough so it would sting, but not hurt, and she really never did hit anybody on the hands.

Instead, aiming her stick at the culprit, she shouted, with great scorn, "You call *that* graceful hands?"

When I knew I was being watched, I could do the most difficult exercises perfectly and they didn't even hurt.

My memories of Frau Dertl are sometimes fond and sometimes painful. While Frau Dertl could be, and often was, gentle, loving, and reassuring, she also had a low level of patience and a bona fide temper. She was a master of withering scorn and sarcasm.

When one of the *élèves* seemed unable to do one of the exercises to her satisfaction, she would, with exquisite courtesy, ask her to watch her. When she had done the exercise with her invariable perfection, and with no apparent effort, she would smile sweetly and in a voice dripping with acid announce:

"If *I* can do it right, as *old* as I am, there is *no* excuse for you."

While she was giving personal attention to a girl who couldn't, or wouldn't, do an exercise to her satisfaction, the rest of the *élèves* had to wait until they were through. At first our sympathies went to the girl, but after a while, we got to be as angry with the lazy one as Frau Dertl was. Or as full of contempt for the inept.

There were even scarcely hidden smiles of satisfaction on innocent eight-year-old faces when Frau Dertl's stick landed on a girl who was holding the class up, and she howled, "Oh, that hurts!"

After a while, Frau Dertl's obviously growing impatience with some of the girls, and the growing complaints by some of the girls about Frau Dertl's abuse of them and the inconveniences of the school generally, made it clear that something was going to have to give. No one was surprised when it did.

One day, at the *barre*, Frau Dertl suddenly shouted rather nastily at the girl next to me: "Get your leg up! *Up! Up! Up!*"

Herr Schnitzer had stopped playing the moment she opened her mouth. The room was silent when we heard the thwack of Frau Dertl's stick on the leg.

"I *can't* get my leg up any further!" the girl screamed back, half angry, half whining.

"There is no such thing as 'I can't'!" Frau Dertl shouted. "You're not trying!"

They glared at one another for a moment and then Frau Dertl knocked her stick on the floor and called out the beat.

The girl didn't move. She had her arms crossed in front of her and her head hung down. The rest of the class watched, horrified. No one had ever openly defied Frau Dertl before.

And then, very calmly, almost conversationally, Frau Dertl said, "Change your clothes and go home. Don't come back!"

The girl looked at Frau Dertl as if she hadn't believed what she heard. And then she suddenly ran across the floor to the dressing room.

Over the next few months the same thing happened with four more girls. Six other girls left voluntarily. Some of them were lazy, but others complained that they just didn't want to do it, at least not every day. They told me that their mothers felt sorry for them.

Ilse did a great deal of complaining, too, but only to me. Nobody else would listen to her. She told me that if she weren't afraid of her mother she would have quit a long time ago.

Once the ones who were either unable or unwilling to tolerate the discipline and the inconveniences of the school had dropped out or been dismissed, the twenty-odd *élèves* left slipped into a routine that seemed somehow to be easier — or at least more pleasant — than the first eight months had been.

Among the girls were three boys. At first I had concluded they were sissies, but then had changed my mind as I saw they worked hard and rarely complained. All three were sons or nephews of principal dancers; they had literally grown up in the Corps de Ballet.

Gradually, I had come to understand this world-unto-itself of ballet: At the lowest level were the *élèves*. At the top were the prima ballerinas and the principal dancers, the ones whose names appeared on the posters and who were genuine celebrities.

Male *élèves* became dancers, and then principal dancers, and then, if not officially, then actually, The Principal Dancer of a Corps de Ballet. Women became dancers, then ballerinas, then The Prima Ballerina.

The ranks were not rigid. A principal dancer or a ballerina might dance a dancer's role in a particular performance, but they were — and everybody knew it — ballerinas and principal dancers nonetheless and they expected to be treated like it.

I was eight when I became an *élève* and just over ten before I was permitted to wear the hard-toed *pointe* slippers of the advanced *élève*.

The atmosphere of the ballet school was such that it came as a surprise, although I later realized that it was according to a long-standing schedule. It had taken two full years of the daily exercises to train our muscles, and, of course, we had grown in the two years since we started training.

Going "on *pointe*" (what most people think of as standing on the toes) places a great stress not only on the toes, but on the muscles of the calf, thigh, and back as well.

When Frau Dertl made her surprise announcement, at the end of one day's routine at the *barre* and on the floor, that we *élèves* were to be given *pointe* slippers the next day, we were ready for them. We had been trained physically and psychologically. Not only weren't we going to hurt our still growing bones by wearing them, but neither did we think of them as anything cute or precious. We knew we had earned the right *to learn* how to use *pointe* slippers in the dance.

Although I had grown accustomed to the discomfort and pain of ballet training generally, I was not prepared for the pain that went with *pointe* slippers.

When I first tried to put them on, Sissy, still my friend and mentor, stopped me.

"They are one size smaller than your soft slippers," she said. "If *pointe* slippers don't fit as tightly as possible, you won't be able to stay on *pointe*."

Sissy began to bend my new slippers in her hands, first upward and then downward. I was surprised that the stitches didn't tear loose. "*Pointe* slippers have to be softened," she said. "You'll have to do this every time before you put them on."

Sissy handed me a ball of cotton wool and showed me how much to pull off. "Two egg-sized balls," she said. The cotton went on top of the toes.

"I have to warn you, Emmy," Sissy said. "This is going to hurt. But only for a moment. The idea is to put the slippers on as quickly as possible. As soon as they are on they stop hurting."

I was willing to be hurt, if that was the price to be paid for wearing *pointe* slippers, but there was another problem.

"Which one is for the right foot?" I asked.

"There's no such thing as right and left *pointe* slippers," Sissy replied.

I jammed my toes into the slipper. The rest of the foot obviously wasn't going to go in as well.

"Put your forefingers in the back, like a shoehorn," Sissy said. "And then give a shove."

Much to my surprise, not only did I get all of my foot into the tiny slipper without tearing the slipper apart, but once I got the foot inside and my fingers out, the pain stopped.

I looked at Sissy triumphantly.

"When you put the other one on, try clenching your teeth," Sissy said. "If you do that, you won't scream."

"Did I scream?" I asked.

Sissy nodded her head. "The quicker you pull your forefingers out, the quicker the pain stops."

I put on the other slipper. This time I

gritted my teeth and pulled my fingers out as quickly as I could. I heard myself groan, but I didn't scream.

I pulled the cord around the top of the slippers tight, tied it, and tucked the ends into the toe. Then I wrapped the straps around my ankles. I put my feet out in front of me and twisted them from side to side as I admired them.

"Come on, Emmy," Sissy urged. "Try them out!"

My first few steps were awkward. The stiffeners in the slippers kept me from walking on the balls of my feet. But after just a few steps I became accustomed to them and walked into the rehearsal hall to the *barre*.

I held onto the *barre* with both hands and then went up on my toes. I stood first on one foot and then the other. I took one hand off the *barre*. And then, afraid of what might happen, the other. Nothing happened.

I was on pointe!

Excited now, I trotted toward the center of the rehearsal hall. I went up on my toes, holding my arms out to the sides to give me balance.

Then Herr Schnitzer began to play. Surprised, I looked at him. He was smiling at me and nodding his head. He was playing for *me!*

To the slow beat of the music, I stood there in the middle of the floor, on *pointe*, taking small steps and turning around, until, no more than a minute later, I became aware of the great strain on my ankles. I dropped off *pointe*. Herr Schnitzer stopped playing. I saw Frau Dertl, and waited for the explosion of her wrath. I had had no permission to do what I had done.

Frau Dertl applauded.

"Very good, Emmy," Frau Dertl said.

But there was always something unpleasant to go with the joyful. When practice was over and I was back in the dressing room, Sissy had the bad news:

"The toe cotton will be stuck to your toes," she said. "Peel it off slowly."

I couldn't understand why the cotton would stick to my toes. When I got the slipper off, I saw the cotton was glued to my toes with blood.

"Don't worry, Emmy," Sissy said, seeing the horror on my face. "After a while there will be less blood and you won't mind it anymore."

Sissy took a damp facecloth from her little case and wiped the blood from my toes. And then she left.

As soon as she was gone, Ilse came over to me.

"I'm not going to put up with this at all!" she announced, on the edge of tears. "I have no intention of crippling my toes!"

I remembered when Ilse had fallen off her toes at the audition, on our first day in the Opera. I could think of nothing to say to her.

"What will your mother say when she finds out about your bloody toes?" Ilse asked.

"I'm not going to tell her," I replied. I had made my mind up about that a moment before. My mother would have had a fit if she saw the blood.

"Well, have it your way! I'm going back to my private school!" Ilse said.

"Ilse, do whatever you want," I said. I was really sick of her whining. If she wasn't willing to pay the price, I had come to believe, she should drop out.

"I'm really going to quit!" Ilse said. I thought it was just one more threat, but it wasn't. Ilse walked out of the dressing room and never came back.

Several months after we *élèves* were given our *pointe* slippers, there were some changes. Sissy and several other advanced *élèves* left to become members of the *First Quadrilles* in the Corps de Ballet (the dancers in the background).

Several more *élèves* dropped out, or were asked to drop out, and what *élèves* were left were promoted to advanced *élèves*.

And on one crisp fall day, my *pointe* slippers wearing a fresh coat of white chalk and new silk ribbons, I — Emmy Macalik, ten-year-old advanced *élève* — swept more than a little smugly down the hall toward the dressing room where one of fifty little girls who didn't even know what a *barre* was, was about to become my student.

Chapter 6

My life was school from eight to two, ballet class from three to five, dinner with my parents at seven, and either homework or listening to records in the living room with Petja on my lap until bedtime, about ten.

Marcella usually came for dinner on Friday and then spent the night, after, sometimes, my parents had taken us to the Opera or the theater or the movies. Saturdays, Marcella and I went to the park, or to the Historical or Natural Art museums.

We liked to go to a coffeehouse, most often the Kaisergarten, on the Ring at Gumpendorferstrasse. We drank black coffee with whipped cream and powdered sugar on top, ate a piece of pastry, and "read" foreign newspapers.

The Kaisergarten, like most large coffeehouses in the center of Vienna, provided foreign newspapers mounted in slotted wooden holders. They were hung up, not unlike pool cues, in a wall rack. We were eleven, and felt quite the women of the world reading (or pretending to) *Paris Match* and the *Times of London* while sipping our coffee.

Marcella was having family trouble. Her father had taken a mistress and moved out of the Jensen apartment. He had installed the mistress in an apartment on the Ringstrasse and was living there. When Marcella visited her father in that apartment, his mistress, of course, was not there, but Marcella saw her clothes and other things and she might as well have been. Marcella confessed that she really hated to go to "that" apartment, and whenever she could she spent her weekends with me and my parents. Life at her mother's apartment was understandably rather sad.

But while I had been living in my new world-of-its-own as an *élève* at the Opera, and as a reader of foreign newspapers in coffeehouses, in the real world the Great Depression had come to Vienna. I hadn't paid any attention to it; it was something that was happening to other people.

One Friday afternoon after ballet class, when I left the Opera to meet Marcella and bring her home with me, my parents were waiting for me outside.

I knew something was wrong. My parents seldom met me, and never both of them together. They took me to the coffeehouse in the Hotel Sacher, on the Philharmonikergasse, right behind the Opera.

I liked the Sacher. It had a Belle Epoque elegance — mirrored walls, glittering chandeliers, and wine red plush upholstery and drapery. When my father picked me up at the Opera, I generally tried to get him to take me there for coffee and pastry and to listen to *Lieder* and operetta melodies played by the tail-coated resident pianist. But today, I sensed that going to the Sacher was something other than a treat.

"We're going to the Sacher to *talk?*" I asked. "Besides," I argued, "I have a rendezvous with Marcella."

I got no answer at all. And when we got to the hotel, after my father ordered for us and while we waited for our coffee, the atmosphere was strained and uncomfortable. My mother was unusually quiet, and her face was as serious and sad as my father's. When the tail-coated waiter finally brought the coffee, my father looked at it as if he didn't know what it was, and then pushed it away.

"I feel very badly about what I have to say to you, Emmy," he said, confirming my suspicions that something was wrong. I thought perhaps I had done something wrong. I looked at my mother. She was playing nervously with her handkerchief and averting her eyes. I wondered if my father was going to tell us that he was leaving us as Marcella's father had; that he, too, had a mistress. Oh, my God, that couldn't be!

"We are living in very bad times," he said,

finally. "More and more people have lost their jobs and many are hungry. You must have seen this yourself."

I shook my head yes. I had, but had no idea what it had to do with me.

"The Depression finally has hit us, too," my father said. "Our family, I mean. And hit us very hard. People have just stopped buying furniture, and Grandfather has had to close the factory." I was relieved. My father was not going to leave us for a mistress.

"What I am trying to tell you, Emmy," he continued, "is that *we* are poor now. I don't have a job, and our money is just about all gone. What I'm trying to tell you is that we can't afford our apartment any longer."

I looked at him in disbelief.

"We moved out today," my father said. I *had* heard him correctly.

"Where are we going to live?" I asked incredulously.

"In a small apartment on Gumpendorferstrasse. About three blocks from where we used to live."

"Why don't we move in with Grandpapa and Grandmama?" I asked. I didn't like the sound of a "small apartment." "They have a big house!" I felt like crying.

"Grandfather has money problems himself," he replied. "Uncle Hubert and his girls are moving in with them. He's going to pay Grandfather rent, and then Grandfather won't lose his house."

I had never liked Uncle Hubert, my father's

older brother. I had liked him even less since his wife had died. I really liked my Aunt Helene. I had once overheard my father telling my mother that Uncle Hubert had a nasty streak in him and that his girls (who were about my age) were spoiled brats.

"We have to be grateful to have a roof over our heads," my father said. "I've been trying hard to find a job, but so have thousands of other men. All I really know is the rattan furniture business, and now there is no rattan furniture business. It's going to be bad, but as long as we're not actually hungry, we can't really complain. Many people, people like us, are in much worse shape."

Was it that bad? Might there not really be enough money for food? That's horrible! Were we *that poor?* I didn't know anybody who was really poor except for our *Hausbesorger.* (When Napoleon occupied Vienna, his military government brought with it the French concierge system: Every apartment building had a concierge — in German, *Hausbesorger* — ostensibly to care for the building and to open the door for tenants late at night. Actually their function was to report anything "suspicious" to the police. When the French left, Emperor Franz Joseph kept the system, but he was never able to turn *Hausbesorgers* into enthusiastic police spies. They became simply people who opened the door late at night and cleaned the building.)

Our *Hausbesorger* and his wife and two children lived on the ground floor of the apartment building. When I forgot my house key and came home after nine o'clock and the front door was locked, I had to ring for the *Hausbesorger* to let me in. My father had always told me to tip him well because he was poor. When the *Hausbesorger*'s children were confirmed, my father and the other people in our apartment building had gotten together to give him the money he needed for the confirmation, the necessary clothing, and for a trip to the Prater.

Were *we* going to be that poor? So poor that someone might give us a few *Schillings* because they felt pity for us?

It wasn't my father's fault. I knew that. It was the Depression. But that didn't change our sad situation. What was I going to do? What was Marcella going to think when she found out? It was nobody's fault, but I was still ashamed.

Then I remembered that Marcella was waiting for me. When I told my father, he gave me ten *Groschen* for the telephone. I called Marcella, blurted that she couldn't come this weekend, or any other one, and then hung up before she could ask any questions. More than anything else, I didn't want Marcella to feel sorry for me.

In the streetcar on the way to the new apartment, I sat between my parents, afraid to ask them what the new apartment was like. They had such sad looks on their faces, I didn't want to make them feel any worse.

We got off one stop further than we normally did and walked down Gumpendorfer-strasse, the next largest street to Mariahil-ferstrasse itself. My father pushed open the big glass entrance door of Number Seventy-two, a five-story stone-faced apartment building. My mother and I followed him in-side, into a large, high-ceilinged entrance hall. The glass door closed automatically, shutting out the sound of a streetcar rattling by.

It was a nice building, I decided, not as nice as the old one, but nice. Maybe it was not going to be as bad as I thought. I followed my parents around a corner to the *Haus-besorger*'s door. My father put a key in the door, opened it, and walked in. My mother followed him. Not quite willing to believe the truth, I followed my mother. Inside was a very small and dark entrance hall. It smelled of mold. I saw the rattan clothesrack, which I had last seen in what had already become the "old apartment." Then I followed my parents through another door into a medium-sized room, almost as dark and as moldy smelling as the entrance hall.

Petja suddenly appeared, barked happily, and jumped up on me. His presence confirmed my worst suspicions: Our new apartment was the *Hausbesorger*'s apartment.

"This is the *Hausbesorger*'s apartment!" I accused.

"This is ours, Emmy," my father said softly, ashamed.

It was, no question about it: There was

79

our kitchen table. There, by a small window, were our chairs. There was Petja's bed, in a dark corner.

I wondered, numbly, if my father was going to open the door for people late at night and take tips. Was my mother going to scrub stairs and halls for other people?

There was one more room, not much larger than the kitchen, with two windows. The floor and the walls were painted the same shade of gray. I couldn't understand why the rooms were so dark. It was still light outside. I went to one of the two windows and saw that it opened onto a small courtyard. I realized that since the *Hausbesorger*'s apartment was at ground level, sunlight was never going to reach those windows unless the sun was directly overhead.

I saw my parents' bed, night tables, wardrobe, and my father's rocking chair. The furniture was too large for the room and hardly left enough place to walk around.

On one of the night tables stood the delicate china ballet dancer, which my father had given me two years before when I began studying piano. I remembered the day he put it on top of my piano. My father saw me looking at it and read my mind.

"Cheer up, Emmy," he said, "we lost the piano, too." He knew how much I hated practicing the piano.

"Where am I going to sleep?" I asked. "Where's my bed?"

My father lifted the quilt on his bed, to

expose a folding bed. It had been under the bed in the guest room in the old apartment. Now it was to be my bed.

I turned away and looked out of the window. I didn't want my parents to see the tears running down my cheeks. Across the small, square cobblestoned courtyard I saw six huge steel garbage cans lined up against the gray stone wall. That was all. There were no trees, no bushes, no birds! Nothing!

I stuck my head out of the window and looked up. More gray stone walls with windows. Only up at the top was a little sliver of blue sky.

Was this how I would live until the Depression was over? What would happen if it lasted for years?

"I've got to get something for supper," my mother said. "Do you want to come with us, Emmy?"

I shook my head no. I didn't want to go anywhere. I didn't want anyone to see me coming out of the *Hausbesorger*'s door.

They left me alone in the bedroom. I stayed at the window, looking out at the garbage cans and remembering the old courtyard with the trees and the birds.

I heard my parents come back, half an hour or so later. But I didn't go to help my mother prepare supper. And then, I heard the doorbell ring and wondered if my mother had been summoned to scrub floors. But it wasn't that.

"Marcella is here," my mother called.

"I don't want to see her, Mama!" I cried.

"I came to pick you up, Emmy," Marcella said from somewhere close by. She sounded as if she wanted to cry, too.

I was ashamed to face her, kept looking out at the garbage cans.

"Olaf is waiting for us," Marcella went on. "He has some new Chopin he wants to play for you."

Marcella was acting as if nothing had happened! As if it made no difference to her that we were poor and living in a *Hausbesorger's* apartment.

I turned around and looked at Marcella. She was petting Petja. She looked up and smiled and motioned with her head for me to come along with her.

I walked out of the apartment with her and tried not to think that I would have to come back.

Chapter 7

The first year in the *Hausbesorger*'s apartment was a bad one. I couldn't get used to our new way of life, and I was terribly ashamed of being poor.

I had previously hated school, but now I was anxious to go each morning because it got me away from home. I spent most weekends at the Jensens' apartment. But my happiest escape from the situation at home was going to the Opera every day.

Often, when I got there, I leaned hard against the heavy side door of the Opera House to close it as quickly as I could, to shut out the world outside, a world I no longer liked.

I didn't think that, except for Uncle Otto, anyone at the Opera knew that I had become, as the Viennese call it, "a *Hausbesorger*'s daughter." The term had all the unfair implications that a racial slur has in America.

Frau Dertl's attitude, if she knew, hadn't changed. She scolded me when I was lazy, and praised me when I'd practiced especially well. The girls and boys didn't seem to treat me any differently, but I was still afraid they knew, or would find out.

It was just before Christmas when Grandmother Macalik suddenly died of a heart attack. My grandfather seemed lost without her, and I missed her, too. Two women I had loved and leaned on were now gone.

Going to the funeral was one of the few times my mother went anywhere. She spent most of her days cleaning the halls and stairs of the building, and spent what free time she had in the kitchen waiting for the bell to ring. She was afraid to leave the building. If she lost her job, we would have no place to live.

When I could, infrequently, on a Sunday afternoon, talk her into going with Petja and me to a nearby park, she became nervous after a few minutes and found some excuse to return to the apartment.

"A light on the staircase might go out. And someone might fall down in the darkness."

Then we had to rush home. My mother was literally terrified of losing the apartment, and her imagination found a vast array of reasons why we could be thrown out.

She dressed simply, and her simple clothing quickly became shabby. I thought my mother looked like the washwoman we used to have. There were no washing machines in the 1930s in Vienna. Washing was done by a washwoman who came once a week to the top-floor laundry room.

My father went out every day, neatly dressed, looking at first for a job and then just for work. When there was a snowstorm, and if he got to the city hiring hall quickly enough, he earned a day's pay shoveling the streets. But that was about all the work there was; there were simply no jobs.

He came home late at night smelling of cheap wine, all he could afford to drink on his unemployment dole, and went quickly to bed.

He didn't do anything wrong when he was drunk, and my mother never upbraided him for his drinking. She seemed to understand that his problems were not of his making and that he was doing all that he could. She understood his frustration at not being able to find work and his humiliation at having to live under a roof that she was providing. Sometimes, however, I heard her quietly crying in the kitchen late at night.

I was grateful to be able to escape the apartment for any reason, but especially grateful for weekends in Marcella's apartment.

The Jensens, as Swedes, were not only not hurt by Austria's Depression, but actually, if unintentionally, profited from it. Marcella's father was attached to the Swedish Embassy and paid in Swedish *kroner*. Swedish money was now more valuable than Austrian *Schil-*

lings and the result of the Austrian Depression was that the Jensens were living better than they would have at home.

So far as they were concerned, food and services in Vienna were dirt cheap. Austria's Depression permitted Marcella's father to support his mistress in one apartment and Marcella, her brother, their mother, and their maid Maria in another.

I spent virtually every weekend at the Jensen apartment. The only good meals I had were at their table. I was treated as one of the family and encouraged to browse in their refrigerator. They took me to the movies, theaters, the Prater, and to the Cobenzl. Every time Marcella got a new dress, I got an identical dress. Frau Jensen and Marcella took great pains not to embarrass me with their kindness.

Several weeks before Christmas 1937, Frau Dertl announced that the *élèves* would be allowed to have their families and friends attend the dress rehearsal of the *Puppenfee* (Fairy Doll), which, since 1888, has been traditionally performed by the Vienna State Opera Corps de Ballet during the Christmas season. I was delighted that I could offer something nice, not only to my parents, but to Frau Jensen, Marcella, and Olaf, too.

On the day of the afternoon dress rehearsal, as we rode on the streetcar to the Opera, I thought how nice my parents looked all dressed up. I had once taken that and so many other things for granted. I didn't anymore. It was the first time I had really seen my mother looking nice or happy in a year.

We arrived at the Opera early, but Marcella and her family were already there. A dress rehearsal was really a private performance for a privileged few. The only difference between a dress rehearsal and a performance was that the auditorium is practically empty for a rehearsal and the best seats in the house are available to whoever wants them. My guests and I took seats in the center of the auditorium, in the tenth row, close enough to really be able to see the stage. In front of the tenth row you have to look up at the stage.

I led Marcella down the aisle to the orchestra pit and introduced her to Uncle Otto.

"Next year," he said, uncommonly gracious to me, "you'll be on the stage for the *Puppenfee*."

I still didn't like Uncle Otto, but had to admit that it had been a very nice thing for him to say. It made me feel good even when we had returned to our seats to wait for the overture and for the curtain to go up.

The *Puppenfee* is about a toy shop, where, at midnight, the toys and dolls suddenly come to life. I knew Sissy was going to dance, but didn't know in what part. Halfway into the first act, I recognized Sissy as one of the wooden soldiers stepping out of their boxes. I nudged Marcella and pointed Sissy out to her. I was proud of Sissy. The wooden soldiers' roles, which required precise and identical movement, were reserved for the better dancers. I was happy for Sissy, and applauded until my hands hurt.

The role of the most beautiful doll, the Puppenfee, is performed by a ballerina. It is the only speaking role in the ballet, just two words. When the Puppenfee called out, in her doll's voice, "Mama, Papa!" I recognized the voice as that of the aunt of one of the boys in my class.

I had been giving Marcella a whispered running commentary on what was going on, and I identified the Puppenfee for her. I could see that she was genuinely impressed with my inside knowledge, and then I realized how much I had become part of all this. I was in the ballet; next year, if I worked very hard, I *would* be dancing in the *Puppenfee* myself.

Uncle Otto and Aunt Anna, whom we hadn't seen since my grandmother's funeral, invited us for Christmas dinner. I had wondered where — or even if — with Grandmother gone, and as poor as we were, we were going to have Christmas dinner.

I was delighted, but my father wasn't at all pleased. As soon as Aunt Anna had left, I heard him talking to my mother.

"If it weren't for Dad, Anna, and Fritz, I wouldn't go. I would just as soon not see Otto or Hubert."

I thought he might be ashamed of not having a job, when they did.

"But it's Christmas," my mother argued. "Be nice, Josef. Let's have a good time."

"Otto will find an excuse to argue, even if it's only about the weather," he replied. "He really behaves as if he's better than the rest of the family. I often wonder why he married Anna; he certainly doesn't like Czechs."

My mother calmed my father down and arranged with the *Hausbesorger* in the next building to stand in for her while we were gone.

Aunt Anna and Uncle Otto lived on the Alserstrasse, a major street in the Eighth Bezirk close to Vienna's largest hospital. Their apartment was as large as the one we had lost. It was on the second floor and had a hand-cranked doorbell under a shiny brass plate with "Schober" engraved on it. When my father turned the doorbell, it made a loud, screeching noise.

My cousin Fritz, who was then eighteen, opened the door, consciously acting the adult. He took our coats and hung them up on a clothesrack, which, like ours, had come from my grandfather's factory, now closed. Uncle Otto didn't care for rattan and the clothesrack was about all there was of rattan furniture in the apartment.

Fritz opened the door to the living room. Two large windows, heavily draped, faced the street, and a Christmas tree heavy with ornaments stood between them.

My cousins Trudy and Hilde stood next to the tree. They waved when they saw me.

Grandfather was sitting on a couch reading the newspaper. Uncle Otto was standing by the piano talking to Uncle Hubert. I went over to my grandfather and kissed him. My father and Uncle Otto shook hands and greeted each other with a joviality even I could see was artificial.

My mother took me into the kitchen. There was the smell of roasting goose, the traditional Viennese Christmas fowl. My Aunt Anna, her face glowing from the heat of the oven, rose from basting the goose. I thought that with my blond wavy hair, I looked very much like my Aunt Anna, who wiped her hands on her apron, hugged and kissed me, and said how happy she was to see me and how pretty my dress was. I hoped she didn't know where I'd gotten it.

I left the kitchen as soon as I could to look for Fritz. I found him lighting candles in the dining room. Two large, silver candelabra, each holding three long red candles, stood on the large table. The table was covered with a lace tablecloth and crowded with china, silver, and crystal. Fritz gave me the matches and let me light the rest of the candles.

Aunt Anna and my mother put biscuits, twisted butter rolls, and several bottles of wine on the table.

"That will do it for now," Aunt Anna said. "Let's join the men for some goose liver. The girls can have Grandmother's raspberry cordial."

The men were standing by a large silver

tray on the piano, helping themselves to pieces of square-cut white bread with goose liver in aspic spread thickly on it.

Uncle Otto poured Hungarian plum brandy, Slivovitz, into glasses and passed them out to the men. Fritz served my mother, Aunt Anna, and us girls raspberry cordial, and then helped himself to a glass of the Slivovitz.

When my grandfather saw what Fritz was drinking, he patted him on his shoulder and jokingly asked him if he planned to get married soon, now that he was man enough to drink strong alcohol. My father teased Fritz about girls, but Fritz didn't seem to mind. He tried to act like an expert on the subject and said that he preferred blondes. The laughter and teasing went on until my grandfather, helping himself to more of the plum brandy, announced the smell from the kitchen had told him it was time to eat.

Uncle Otto rather formally went and opened the door into the dining room. Except for my mother and Aunt Anna, everyone followed him to the dining table.

Aunt Anna and my mother then served the goose and other hot food. The table reminded me of other meals at my grandmother's table at Christmas. Everything was there: the steaming, golden brown goose surrounded by bowls of dumplings, roasted potatoes, white asparagus, French-style green beans, mushroom gravy, and warm cabbage salad.

Uncle Otto sat at the head of the table. My cousins Trudy and Hilde sat on either side of him; Aunt Anna sat at the foot of the table with my father on one side and me on the other; Uncle Hubert and my mother sat on the right side of the table, and my grandfather and Fritz on the left.

Everyone bowed their heads for the customary prayer of thanks. I was sorry to see that Uncle Otto was going to do the praying. He was never satisfied with a simple expression of gratitude to the Almighty for His gifts. Giving thanks before a meal always gave him the opportunity to make a speech. I didn't pay much attention to what he said, but was aware that he was taking as long as I was afraid he would. Immediately after the "Amens" I heard Aunt Anna ask for the wine.

And then I heard my father say, sadly, not angrily:

"The next time, Otto, leave me out of that 'unify us with our fatherland' business."

"Josef!" My mother, alarmed, tried to shush him.

I remembered hearing something like that during Uncle Otto's lengthy prayer. I hadn't known what he meant, but I hadn't known the meaning of half of what he had said.

"All right," Uncle Otto said, and he was very jovial, but there was something cold in his voice. "It's going to happen anyway, whether or not I pray for it, and whether or not you like it."

"I pray to God it doesn't," my father said, and he wasn't even trying to be pleasant.

"I don't understand you at all, Josef,"

92

Uncle Otto said to him as if he were a child. "What do you want? To stay on the unemployed dole?"

"Otto," Aunt Anna protested, "that was cruel!"

"Not at all," Uncle Otto said, confidently. "It's the truth. The only thing that's going to get Josef a job is National Socialism, and the only way we're going to get National Socialism is to unite with Germany, and the only way we're going to be able to do that is through Adolf Hitler."

"Not at dinner," Aunt Anna said. "Not at a family dinner."

"Your violin-playing husband, Anna, and a Männerheim inmate [the Männerheim was Vienna's refuge of last resort for unemployed men who were totally without assets], an upper Austrian *petit bourgeois* [Viennese felt vastly superior to upper Austrians, regarding them, if unfairly, as dull, plodding peasants], are going to lead us, like Moses, to the promised land," my father said.

"Why don't you say 'just a corporal,' too?" Uncle Otto said.

"All right," my father said. "An upper Austrian *petit bourgeois* corporal is going to lead us to the land of milk and honey. And in the meantime, turn us all into Germans. That's the real miracle. I don't have one drop of German blood in me, but he's going to make me into a German."

"We are a German people," Uncle Otto said formally.

"We may be as crazy as the Germans," my father said. "But you're no more a German than your man Hitler is. You don't have any more German blood in you than I do. Than Herr Hitler does."

"Crazy! Crazy! When the National Socialists came to power, Germany was flat on its back, humiliated before the world, about to be taken over by the Communists. Now look at it!" Uncle Otto said loudly.

"That's what I mean by being crazy," my father said.

"People in Germany have jobs," Uncle Otto said. "Tell me that's not true."

I expected a reply to that from my father, but he made none. There was an awkward silence for a while, as the goose was carved and served.

"You'll see, Josef," Uncle Otto said placatingly. "Things will be better. The trouble with you is that you read too many newspapers, and the newspapers are all owned by the Jews."

"The Jews are responsible for the Depression?" my father replied. "Funny, I always thought it was the Versailles Treaty."

"International Jewry," Uncle Otto said flatly.

"Then how do you explain the Jews in line beside me at the Unemployment Office?" my father asked.

"You can't argue with people who have eyes but won't see," Uncle Otto said.

"I agree," my father said. "I agree."

Uncle Otto's face grew red.

"Would you rather have the Communists, Josef?"

"I would rather be left alone," my father said. "I don't really care what happens in Germany. If they are foolish enough to let Hitler take over, that's their business. I just don't want him, and those clowns in brown shirts, to take over Austria."

"Clowns in brown shirts?" Uncle Otto asked, but my father wasn't listening, and he went on:

"What really baffles me is how he has so many people who should know better, intelligent people, jumping like marionettes when he pulls their strings."

"Intelligent people?" Uncle Otto said. "Thank you, Josef."

My father chuckled. He didn't say anything, but Uncle Otto must have caught his meaning, for even I knew that when he said "intelligent people" he wasn't thinking of Uncle Otto.

"Adolf Hitler," Uncle Otto said, "and the National Socialist Party could not have come to power in Germany without the support of all the people, the peasants, the bourgoisie, the intelligentsia, and the aristocracy."

"Adolf Hitler," my father said, "who could never hold a job in his life, came to power at the head of a mob of roughnecks and social misfits and —"

"Social misfits?" Uncle Otto interrupted him icily.

"So-called aristocrats and noblemen," my father went on, "who would like to get their lands and castles back."

"You think I'm a social misfit?" Uncle Otto demanded.

"I think you're a musician who knows absolutely nothing about either economics or politics," my father said.

"And you do?"

"I know enough about economics to know that you can't cure a depression by marching around in a brown shirt blaming it on the Jews," my father said.

"You're a fool, Josef!" Uncle Otto said, suddenly losing his temper.

"That's enough!" my grandfather said suddenly, even more angry than Uncle Otto. "I will hear no more of this at my table! This is *Christmas Dinner!*"

There was silence for a long moment. Aunt Anna broke it. "Pass the bowls around before everything gets cold," she said, artificially jovial.

When dinner was over, everyone went into the living room for chocolate cake and very strong coffee served in tiny cups and saucers and cognac afterward, for the adults.

While the adults drank their cognac, Aunt Anna gave my cousins Trudy and Hilde and me our Christmas presents: leather handbags with a separate coin purse. There was money in my coin purse.

I was happy with my present, but felt uncomfortable. There was a tense atmosphere in the room. My mother tried to start a conversation, but it soon died. And when my grandfather said something intended to be funny, the dutiful laughter was strained.

I was glad when my father announced that it was getting late and we would have to go home. Aunt Anna kissed everyone, and said how pleased she was to have had the whole family.

Without that fighting over Herr Hitler, whoever he was, I thought, it would have been a perfect Christmas Day.

Chapter 8

On New Year's Day, Vienna's chimney sweeps pin white carnations to the lapels of their working uniforms (a coal-dust-soaked suit and a top hat) and call on all of their customers to wish them a Happy New Year. They are confident of a healthy tip, because Viennese believe that touching chimney sweeps brings good luck, and few people will pass up the chance to get a little extra good luck.

For the very good reason that *Hausbesorgers* cannot afford to tip, chimney sweeps don't trouble to wish *Hausbesorgers* a Happy New Year.

I waited for the chimney sweep in the foyer. He glanced at me and started up the stairs. I gathered my courage, ran after him, and touched him. Whether I could afford it or not, I knew I needed a little good luck. He turned around, smiled, and wished me Happy New Year.

During the holiday season, I had begun to

hear more and more about Hitler. Everyone was talking about him and the Nazis. (The word *Nazi* is an acronym for *National Sozialistische Deutsche Arbeiter Partei*, National Socialist German Workers' Party.) The nuns and priests at school all seemed convinced that Hitler and the Nazis were going to bring better times to Austria. They said after the Nazis had come to power in Germany, Hitler had provided jobs and ended the Depression. As soon as Hitler came to Austria, they said, there would be jobs and the Depression would end here, too.

I couldn't forget the fight my father had had with Uncle Otto at Christmas dinner over Hitler, but thought my teachers couldn't be *that* wrong. After all, they were *teachers*! Maybe my father was mistaken.

I wanted to ask him about it, but when he came home, late at night, he had usually been drinking, and I couldn't talk to him. One Sunday morning, however, there was the opportunity to ask him about what my teachers had said about Hitler.

"Emmy, you're probably not old enough to understand," he said seriously. "But I *know* about Hitler. He is crazy and so are his followers. He is an uneducated man who has surrounded himself with thugs. The only thing he can really do well is give a speech. I think he's absolutely no good and probably very dangerous, but he's got Uncle Otto, and your teachers, and just about everybody else convinced that he's the salvation of Germany and Austria."

I decided I couldn't get anywhere arguing with my father about Herr Hitler. As far as I was concerned, however, Herr Hitler was going to bring me luck and end the Depression. Just about everybody but my father said they couldn't wait for Hitler to come to Vienna.

He came, two months later, on March 14, 1938.

I was let out of school for the great occasion, *"Den Anschluss zum Deutschen Reich"* (the incorporation of Austria into the German Reich as the province of Ostmark). The city government decreed a three-day holiday to celebrate.

Radio Vienna announced there was going to be a big parade. It would begin at the Westbahnhof, Vienna's largest railroad station, and move down Mariahilferstrasse to the Ring, and then down the Ring to the Imperial Hotel, a block past the Opera.

On the morning of the great day, when the radio in the kitchen confirmed the time the parade was going to start, I decided I had to go, even though my parents had forbidden me to do so. I told them I was going to the park around the corner.

On Mariahilferstrasse there was a contagious atmosphere of joy, even ecstasy; it quickly infected me, too. I had never seen so many happy people in my life! Everyone was laughing and chattering with excitement.

Some people carried fresh-cut flowers in their hands and others held small flags. Some of the flags were Austrian (three horizontal stripes — red, white, and red), but most were Nazi flags, a black swastika in a white circle on a red flag.

The street was decorated even more colorfully than for the Easter parade, which normally, in Roman Catholic Austria, was the most gala annual event. Large flags hung from apartment buildings, either flat against the building or from flag poles pointing out over the street. Long banners hung from the lamp poles. Even the churches flew huge Austrian and German flags. Many, perhaps most, windows displayed large color portraits of Hitler. Vases of cut flowers had been placed beside them.

An area of Mariahilferstrasse as wide as the streetcar tracks was blocked off by long lines of smiling policemen. They kept the crowds back by forming a human chain, their arms locked together.

Many of the older men in the crowd wore their First World War uniforms, and other men, who hadn't kept their uniforms, wore their war medals pinned to the lapels of their jackets. Many, again probably most, of the younger men wore red Nazi swastika armbands.

As I was carried along in the crush of the crowd, someone put a small Nazi flag into my hand. I would have waved it if I could have moved my arms.

People linked arms and began to sing, swaying in unison in time with the music very much like the patrons full of wine in Vienna Woods wine bars. The whole atmosphere reminded me of the Fasching (Vienna's equivalent of Mardi Gras in New Orleans), where people sing and dance in the street.

From the direction of the West railroad station, I could hear a swelling roar and much cheering. The sound came closer and closer and then I could hear military march music over it. A large military band had marched by. The people cheered, waved their flags, and threw flowers. When I was able to free my arm, I waved my swastika flag, too.

Behind the band came wide ranks of soldiers in brown uniforms. They were greeted with shouts of "Heil Hitler! Heil Hitler!" The soldiers, many of whom wore flowers pinned to their tunics and taped to their steel helmets, smiled and waved at the spectators.

The cheering became even louder. A big, black, open car crowded with fat officers passed us. And then another. The third open car, an enormous open Mercedes-Benz convertible sedan with a swastika flag flying on the front fender, carried a brown-uniformed man standing up in the front seat holding onto the windshield. He looked just like his pictures in the store windows. Adolf Hitler! The Leader! He rode by expressionlessly, neither smiling nor waving at the crowd.

People jumped up to get a better view of

him, waving their flags and throwing flowers onto his car. A man next to me landed heavily on my foot.

"Heil Hitler! Heil Hitler!" gave way to just a mindless litany, from a hundred thousand voices, of "Hit-ler! Hit-ler! Hit-ler!"

Then people around me asked each other excitedly, "Did you see him? Did you see him?"

After the last car in the procession, there were more marching soldiers. When the last row of these had passed, the policemen broke their human chain. Everybody began to follow the parade.

I didn't want to go. My foot hurt, and I didn't want to walk all the way back home from the Imperial Hotel, where Hitler was going. It was a big block beyond the Opera. Furthermore, with all the commotion on the streets, my mother was sure to look for me in the park. If she did, she would find out I'd disobeyed her and gone to the parade.

But I couldn't get out of the crowd. I was trapped in the huge mob of people filling Mariahilferstrasse from one side to the other all the way to the Ring. I was literally carried along in the mob all the way to the Ring, and then down the Ring to the Opera.

I ended up in the middle of an even more tightly packed group of people in front of the Imperial Hotel. Two buttons were missing from my blouse, my skirt was torn, my hair was messed up, and my foot was now painfully swollen.

Everyone was looking up at the hotel, where an enormous swastika had been hung from a balcony over the main entrance. The crowd, their voices now hoarse, had begun to shout over and over, "We won't go home! We won't go home till the *Führer* speaks!"

Most of them were still waving flags. Mine had been torn from my hands a long time ago, but I wouldn't have waved it anymore anyway. I had had enough of the whole thing. I wished that Hitler would hurry and show up on the balcony and speak. Then the people would break up and I could go home.

When Hitler didn't show up, I began to panic. I started to push at the people who stood around me in an attempt to get away. I knew if I could get to the sidewalk I could then get around a corner and into a side street. They didn't notice, even as hard as I shoved. That made me push even harder. I pushed and kicked my way through the crowd and finally reached the sidewalk.

From the relative safety of an alley, I saw people sitting on the branches of the chestnut trees on the Ring. And I saw a woman and a small child being carried away in an ambulance.

I went farther down the alley, and eventually got away from the crowd. I was sweaty and had a headache. My swollen foot hurt so badly that I took off my shoe and carried it in my hand as I ran toward home. It was a long way and it was almost dark when I finally got back to the apartment.

I examined myself as well as I could in the mirror on the rattan clothesrack in the dark foyer. I looked terrible! As if I had been in a fight. Which is exactly what I told my mother. She didn't like to hear that I had been fighting, but she let it pass. My mother was more concerned about my father, who had had "a little too much to drink" again.

My father stayed that way, dead drunk, until the three-day *Anschluss* holiday was over.

Chapter 9

I knew only a few Jews. Herr Stein, our dentist, who had often come with his wife to dinner in our old apartment, was a Jew. When he set aside a corner of his waiting room for small children, my father had had the factory make a special, child-sized set of brightly colored rattan furniture for it.

When we moved into the *Hausbesorger*'s apartment, Herr Stein had tactfully told my father to make sure I visited him regularly; he could settle the accounts when "things got better."

Then there was Herr Goldberg, who owned a clothing store on Mariahilferstrasse where we had often shopped. When my parents had taken me there to select birthday clothing, Herr Goldberg had always wrapped "a little extra," like a scarf or gloves, in the package for me.

And then there were the Spinats, who had an apartment in our new building. Herr

Spinat owned a jewelry store on Kärntner-strasse, Vienna's Fifth Avenue. Frau Spinat often had coffee with my mother in the *Hausbesorger* apartment kitchen, and I often carried her packages to their third-floor apartment.

Frau Spinat loved to bake and I was always treated to a piece of her cake and coffee.

The Spinats loved the ballet and sometimes I danced for them in the evening. I had told Frau Spinat about Frau Fischer, Herr Strauss, and their two friends. When I visited Frau Spinat, she invariably gave me some delicatessen (literally, delicate things to eat), which we could no longer afford, to take home, and Herr Spinat frequently put money in my pocket, saying, "Don't tell your mother, Emmy!"

These were my Jews, my Semites. They were perfectly ordinary people. There had been anti-Semitism before Hitler came, but it had never touched me, or anybody I knew, including "my" Jews. Now it was not only respectable to be anti-Semitic, but expected of good Viennese. The underlying cruelty was that until Nazi-sponsored anti-Semitism affected them, most Jews had thought of themselves as Viennese who happened to be Jewish.

The Nazis, of course, thought differently: Herr Goldberg's plate glass store windows were painted in large white letters: "Jew! Don't buy here!"

I saw Jews pushed — or kicked — off the sidewalks.

I didn't understand why the Nazis did this to people like the Goldbergs. To me, a Jew was a man who had a long black beard, wore a black hat, a black suit, and, even in warm weather, a long black coat. But Herr Stein, Herr Goldberg, and the Spinats were people like myself. I asked my father why the Nazis, and some people who weren't Nazis, hated the Jews.

"The Nazis are mostly lower-class people, Emmy," my father told me. "This is the first time they've ever had a chance to push anybody around. And some of them are thugs who have been in and out of jails. You can put a thug in a uniform, but he's still a thug."

One morning when I returned from buying leftover rolls (they were a little stale, but were half price), Frau Spinat was sitting in our kitchen. I was surprised to see her so early in the morning.

"Would you like a roll, Frau Spinat?" I asked.

"No thank you, darling," Frau Spinat said. She and my mother seemed to be preoccupied.

"Is there anything I can help you with?" my mother asked Frau Spinat, obviously returning to a conversation I had interrupted.

"There isn't much we can take. Just the two suitcases," Frau Spinat replied.

"Are you going on a holiday, Frau Spinat?" I asked.

"Sort of a holiday, Emmy," she said, with a faint smile.

My mother put her finger to her mouth in a signal for me to shut up.

"I'll miss chatting with you," Frau Spinat said to my mother. Then she stood up and hugged me. "I'll especially miss you, Emmy." I could see Frau Spinat was on the edge of crying. Then she quickly left the apartment.

"What's wrong with Frau Spinat?" I asked as soon as she had gone.

"Nothing that concerns you," my mother replied, and found some way to change the subject.

The next morning my parents and I went to the Spinats' apartment to say good-bye. The Spinats' eyes were red and swollen as if they had been crying. When they went into the living room, Frau Spinat led me to the crystal vase on her piano.

"You've often told me of Frau Fischer's vase, Emmy," Frau Spinat said. "I want you to have this one." She handed it to me.

I thought that Frau Spinat wanted me to keep the vase for her until she returned from her trip.

"I'll take good care of it," I said.

I saw that my mother looked as though she wanted to cry, and so did Frau and Herr Spinat. I couldn't understand why they were so upset. Most wealthy Viennese got out of the hot city in the summer.

"The taxi is here, Herr Spinat," my father

said, looking out the window. "We must leave." He picked up the two suitcases and carried them out onto the street. The taxi driver took the suitcases from him and put them into the trunk.

Herr Spinat started to help his wife into the taxi, but she stopped in front of the door and looked up at the apartment building. Herr Spinat put his arm around her shoulder and gently pushed her into the taxi. Then my father got into the taxi after the Spinats.

"You shouldn't come with us," Herr Spinat said.

"I'll put you on the train," my father said firmly.

The Spinats waved at my mother and me and we waved back until we couldn't see the taxicab any longer. I saw that my mother behaved strangely when we returned to the apartment: She seemed nervous and worried. First, she burned her hand making coffee, and then she dropped a cup and saucer and didn't seem to really notice. I wondered what was wrong with her.

When my father returned from the railroad station and my mother asked him if everything had gone all right, her voice was frightened, and she was obviously relieved to hear that the Spinats had gotten away without trouble. Nothing else was said about the Spinats after that.

A week or so later the postman knocked on our door and handed me a postcard. I was surprised; we got little mail, and he seldom came to the *Hausbesorger*'s door except to leave a package for a tenant who wasn't at home. The postcard had a color picture of Buckingham Palace on one side. I turned it over. There was an English stamp on the other side, and a brief message in German: "Enjoying London. Best wishes. Schmidt."

It was very strange. As far as I knew, we didn't know anybody by the name of Schmidt. For that matter, we didn't know anybody in London, either.

"Who are the Schmidts, Papa?" I asked, when I handed him the card.

"Thank God!" my father said, snatching the card from my hand. "They made it!"

"Who made what?" I asked curiously.

"The Spinats are safe in England," my father said.

"Safe from what?"

"The Spinats didn't go on a vacation, Emmy," he explained. "They left Austria for good. So they wouldn't 'vanish' the way some other Jewish families have already vanished."

"You're talking about the Nazis, aren't you?" I asked. He nodded his head. "Why would the Nazis harm the Spinats?" I pursued.

He shrugged his shoulders helplessly.

"It cost the Spinats everything they'd ever worked for," my father said. "But at least they're safe. They're alive."

"They had to leave everything behind?" I asked. "Is that why Frau Spinat gave me the vase?"

"If the Spinats hadn't 'sold' everything they owned to the Nazis for a *Groschen* [penny] on the *Schilling*, they wouldn't have been allowed to leave Vienna," my father explained.

"Everything? The store, too? The apartment?"

"Everything," my father said. He looked at his hands. They were balled into tight fists, and the knuckles were white. A moment later, with an effort, he unclenched them.

"Go up to the Spinats' apartment and help your mother," he said. "She really feels bad having to clean it for the new people."

The new people who moved into the Spinats' apartment a week later were Nazis. Herr Müller was a chubby little man with a red nose who wore his Army captain's uniform with great pride. My father said that he looked like a Frenchman who drank too much cheap wine. Frau Müller was skinny and much taller than her husband. She was never without her Nazi Party brooch proudly pinned to her chest.

The Müllers had twin eight-year-old boys and a girl my age. The boys most often wore their Hitler Youth uniforms and their sister her BDM (the acronym for *B*und *D*eutscher *M*ädel, or Organization of German Girls) uniform.

Going up or down the stairs from their

apartment, the Müller children were noisy. When other tenants complained about them to my mother and she went to Frau Müller with the complaints, Frau Müller just laughed at her.

Every time we saw Frau Müller and her children, they greeted us with "Heil Hitler!" and her husband walked past us as if we were invisible.

One morning when my father and I walked out of our apartment, we met Frau Müller and her three children in the foyer.

"Heil Hitler!" all four of them cried in unison.

"*Grüss Gott*," my father replied calmly, offering the traditional Viennese greeting.

Nazis expected to get a "Heil Hitler" reply when they gave that greeting, and considered it a personal affront if they didn't. I was afraid of what might happen. But Frau Müller merely gave my father a dirty, if superior, look and walked by us. Her children stuck out their tongues. My father smiled warmly back at them.

My father did get a job. After proving that he was an Aryan and entitled to a job in the New Germany, he got a job as a courier for the State Bank, carrying securities from Vienna to banks all over Germany.

We moved out of the *Hausbesorger*'s apartment into an apartment on the top floor of the same building. It wasn't as large as the one we had had before the Great De-

pression, but it was as different as day from
night to the *Hausbesorger*'s apartment. I had
my own room again and could see the sky
from my window. There were even flower
pots on the windowsills as we used to have.
Most of our old furniture had been sold, but
my grandfather had a stock of unsold furniture from the rattan factory stored in his
attic, and he gave us what we needed.

My father cut down on his drinking, and
was most often at home at night. He said
most people were not worth talking to anymore, but it was more than that, and I knew
it. I knew that my father was afraid that if
he drank in public, his tongue would loosen
and get him in trouble.

I knew, although I wasn't supposed to, how
bad he felt about the Steins. I suspected, but
didn't know for sure, that Herr Stein had
regularly given my father money during our
bad times. I knew that the first Saturday we
were in the new apartment, he had gone to
see the Steins to ask them to come for Sunday
dinner.

When he returned, he had looked terrible.
His face was gray. My mother asked him if
he was sick. He didn't answer her, but
waved me out of the room. I closed the door
but put my ear against it. When I heard my
father crying bitterly, I had opened the door
a crack and looked in.

He was sitting in his rocking chair, and my
mother was holding him. When he gained

control of himself, he wiped his eyes with a handkerchief.

"When I couldn't get an answer at the Steins," he said, "I went to the *Hausbesorger*. He told me that the Gestapo came ten days ago. They took the Steins, the little boy, too. Nobody has heard from them since."

My parents never mentioned the Steins again. And I was afraid to.

Chapter 10

The *Puppenfee* Ballet was as much a part of Christmas in Vienna as Christmas trees and Saint Nicholas. For students in the Corps de Ballet at the Opera, it had a special significance, for it was the vehicle used to give advanced *élèves* their first opportunity to perform before a paying audience.

Some of the "performances" were nothing more than sitting on a shelf of the toy shop set in the first act. But this gave the young dancers the experience of being costumed and made up, and the emotional shock of being on stage. When the curtain went up, the eyes of everyone in the invariably packed auditorium were on whoever was on the stage, even if the performers were under strict orders to just sit there, without a suggestion of a wiggle.

There were legitimate dancing roles in the second act, where the dolls and wooden soldiers in the toy shop come to life. The role of the Fairy Doll herself was performed by a ballerina, and principal dancers danced five of the six National Doll roles.

The National Dolls, representing the nationalities of the old Austro-Hungarian Empire, are costumed in the regional dress of Hungary, Slovakia, and so on. The role of the Austrian Doll, who wears a Tyrolean costume, is traditionally given to an advanced *élève* of exceptional promise.

Every little girl in the ballet school dreamed that a miracle would happen, that every dancer better than she would break a leg or come down with mumps or the measles, leaving no one else to dance the Austrian Doll.

That was fantasy. Reality was desperately hoping to get your name on the list to sit on a toy shop shelf in Act One. Not every advanced *élève* was to be that lucky. Happiness on Earth was to be selected to dance one of the tiny roles in Act One.

The *Puppenfee* was not like the recitals in private ballet schools, where any child whose parents could come up with the tuition was guaranteed a chance to strut her stuff. These were performances of the Corps de Ballet of the Vienna State Opera. The audience would be people who had paid real money, and who would expect a real performance.

Actually, it was even worse than that. All Viennese devoutly believe that they are born with a knowledge of music and the ballet that obliges them to seek out and criticize the slightest mistake in any performance of the Philharmonic, the Opera, or the Ballet. They are aided in their criticism by the professional critics of the press, who very rarely find any performance by anyone as good as it should be.

When it comes to something like a performance of Beethoven's Fifth Symphony, or Verdi's *Aida*, or the *Puppenfee*, works that most of the audience have just about memorized, the State Opera audience waits to pounce on mistakes like a hungry dog eyeing a large bone.

We all knew the schedule, when those of us considered good enough to sit on the toy shop shelves would be named, and when the rest of us, having been judged and found wanting, would go off somewhere and try not to show how much it hurt.

Whatever I was, I was not a modest little girl. I might not get to dance a few steps and make a few turns without going on *pointe* in Act One, but there was no question in my mind that I had earned the right to sit, suitably made up and in costume, on a toy shop shelf. Except for the times at practice when Frau Dertl yelled at me because I wasn't paying attention, I thought I did well, and couldn't see any reason why I wouldn't be selected to sit on a shelf, and, conceivably, to dance.

By the middle of October, however, when it was time for Frau Dertl to announce her choices, I had lost much of my self-confidence. Instead of anxiously waiting for the announcement, I wished that it would be made sometime later, say next year. Every time I pushed open the big door to enter the Opera, I was afraid that today was going to be the day.

And one day, it was. Frau Dertl called us all together after practice and said she had several announcements to make. When I saw her pick up a sheet of paper, obviously the list of the chosen, I was able to quickly change my mind and decide that it really didn't matter that I would be one of the rejects. Deep in my heart, I hadn't really worked hard enough throughout the year. I didn't deserve to be on the list of the chosen. Next year would be something else.

Frau Dertl began to call out names of girls and boys who would have small roles in the first act. They would be the baby dolls and the rag dolls, the teddy bears, and the other shelf sitters.

Although I had steeled myself for it, I was very disappointed when my name wasn't called. I had lost my chance to be in the *Puppenfee*. With an absolutely hypocritical (and probably wholly transparent) smile on my face, I forced myself to congratulate those who had made it.

"For the part of the Austrian Doll," Frau Dertl went on, "I had quite a problem."

I hope the problem is a broken leg *and* mumps, I thought.

"But we finally decided that Emmy Macalik should have it," Frau Dertl finished.

For a moment, I couldn't believe I had heard right. Did she really say *my* name or was I just dreaming? But then the rest of the class started to scream and run toward me. In a moment, little girls who probably meant it were hugging me and telling me they were happy for me.

"Silence, please!" Frau Dertl called. It took a while before everybody calmed down. Then she continued, "For those of you that missed out, all I can say is that there's always next Christmas and the next *Puppenfee.*"

I didn't believe that at all. This year's *Puppenfee* was not going to be like any other *Puppenfee.* This was *my Puppenfee.*

The next day the doll box was brought into the rehearsal room. It was a wooden crate in the shape of a doll box, painted white, and large enough to hold a dancer.

When the rest of the class had been dismissed, I was told to stay and Frau Dertl began to explain what was expected of me. She led me to the box, handed me the white stiff cardboard lid, and showed me how to hold it in place so the audience couldn't see me, until the musical cue to come out was played.

Then, with Herr Schnitzer playing a Johann Strauss waltz, Frau Dertl demonstrated what steps I would be making:

I was first to make a fast *rond de jambe* on *pointe* with my right leg, touching the floor on *pointe,* and then with my left leg.

Then I was to make a complete turn on *pointe* simultaneously moving one arm above my head, then raising the other arm, and ending with both arms down in front.

The fast *rond de jambe* was then repeated four times, this time with my legs raised to hip level, and followed by four complete turns on *pointe.*

The last movement was the *développé.* I would do it six times, followed by six complete turns, and then I was to finish with a *reverence* (deep bow).

Until the day of the dress rehearsal, I practiced an additional hour each day after regular practice with my class. From the first session, I began to wonder if I hadn't bitten off more than I could hope to chew. As the dress rehearsal and the performance drew closer, there was no question in my mind that I had. An hour a day didn't seem nearly long enough to memorize the steps, much less to learn to do them perfectly.

The day of the dress rehearsal came much too quickly, long before I had acquired anything like confidence in my role.

When I arrived in the dressing room at noon, three hours before the performance, carrying my *pointe* slippers in my small leather bag, the five elderly assistant wardrobe mistresses were already carrying as many costumes as they could hold in their arms and passing them out to the dancers.

I looked for Frau Hartmann, the wardrobe

mistress who had fitted me into my costume
two weeks before. She had told me that she
had been a wardrobe mistress for the Corps
de Ballet for more than thirty years. She had
promised to dress me. I spotted her and
headed for her, but just as I reached her, a
dancer, much older than I, called out:

"Frau Hartmann, help me, please! My
seam is open!"

"Right away, *Liebchen*!" Frau Hartmann
replied, but she came to me instead, told me
to undress, and disappeared. She returned
shortly afterward carrying my costume in
her arms as gently as she would have carried
a baby.

"Put the petticoats on, *Liebchen*. I'll be
right back," she said, handing them to me.
Then she hurried over to the dancer with
the popped seam, calling out, "I'm coming,
Liebchen!"

There were three white, stiffly starched
petticoats. I put the first one on and tied the
two white ribbons at the waist in a small
bow. Then I turned it around so that the ribbons would be in the back. I remembered
Frau Hartmann's doing it that way. The
petticoat was as short as, and stood out like,
a tutu. I put on the other two petticoats.

The blouse had short, unusually large,
heavily starched sleeves, puffed out like bal-
loons. Since Frau Hartmann hadn't returned,
I put it on. The buttons were tiny, and there
were so many of them that I had a difficult
time closing all of them.

"Sorry to make you wait, *Liebchen*," Frau Hartmann said, running up to me.

She pulled a brightly colored flower-print jumper, only slightly shorter than the petticoats, over my head. The jumper laced in front with a long ribbon, very much like a high-laced shoe.

Frau Hartmann pulled the ribbon tight, tied the ends at the waist in a bow, and took a few steps back. She put her hand to her cheek, then shook her head in disapproval.

"We *must* have more petticoats, *Liebchen*," she announced, and scurried off.

Another petticoat? I already had three. I realized that what Frau Hartmann was trying to do was make the skirt of the Austrian national costume, the *Dirndl*, look even more like a dancer's tutu. The more petticoats, the more the skirt would stick out.

After I had put on a fourth and then a fifth petticoat, Frau Hartmann was apparently satisfied, because she then tied a tiny, bright red apron with a heavily starched bow in the back over the jumper, carefully adjusting the apron strings so they exactly reached the hem of the jumper.

"Now you look like an Austrian doll! Good luck, *Liebchen*!" she cried, kissed me on my cheek, and rushed off to another dancer, calling out, "I'm coming, *Liebchen*!"

I was so excited that I forgot my slippers and walked out of the dressing room barefooted. Another dancer, laughing, let me know by pointing at my feet. Embarrassed, I returned to the dressing room for my new pink *pointe* slippers. I had worn them only enough to soften them: I was saving them for to-night.

Then I went down the hall to the makeup room, which looked like a large beauty shop without hairdryers. I looked at the unreal face of a dancer who was already made up. Her skin was brown, and her cheeks were bright red. Was she really going to go on the stage looking like that?

A woman wearing the pink cotton smock of the makeup department asked for my name, and then pointed to a dancer having her hair done at one of the makeup tables.

"You're after her," she said.

Ten minutes later the pink-jacketed makeup man working on her finished and waved me into his chair. He put a huge oilcloth cover over me and turned to his makeup table. An imposing display of makeup, in different sizes and colors of jars, filled a work surface in front of a large mirror framed with small round light bulbs.

"I haven't seen you here before," the makeup man said as he framed my face with sticky-backed tissue paper. "First time?"

I nodded.

"And you're afraid, right?" he said. "A little stage fright?"

"A little."

"Don't worry, *Liebchen*," he said, smiling. "*Everybody* has stage fright. Even the old-timers. It's normal."

124

He gently dabbed brown cream on my face. Then he painted my cheeks bright red. As I watched in the brightly lit mirror, I saw that I was going to look just like the dancer I had seen before.

He told me to close my eyes. I felt something soft, like cotton, on my face, then what felt like a soft brush.

"If you don't want to get this in your eyes," he said, "keep them closed, and hold still."

I felt his gently rubbing finger on my eyelids, and then felt something brush my eyelashes.

When he finally told me I could open my eyes and I could look in the mirror, my eyes looked to be at least three times their normal size. My eyelids were green, and huge false black eyelashes had been glued onto my real ones. My eyebrows had been painted large and black. All things considered, however, I liked the way my eyes looked.

"Now hold still and open your mouth a little," the makeup man said. He picked up a small jar of red cream, dipped his little finger in it, and smeared it onto my lips. Then he took a red grease pencil and carefully drew a line on the outside of them.

"How do you like yourself now?" he asked.

"I don't know," I answered truthfully.

"If you went before the footlights without makeup, you would look like a corpse," the makeup man said. He peeled the tissue paper off. I thought that meant he was finished, but when I tried to get up, he pushed me back into the chair.

"Just sit there, *Liebchen*," he said. "I'll be right back."

He returned with a nearly yellow blond wig on its storage head. Braided pigtails as long and at least twice as wide as mine hung down on both sides.

"Okay," he said. "That's it."

When I looked in the mirror, I thought that the girl in the Austrian Doll costume looked very pretty even if no one in the world was going to recognize her as Emmy Macalik.

Back in the dressing room I sat down next to Sissy.

"Scared, Emmy?" Sissy asked.

I nodded. Now that it was getting close to curtain time, I was so scared I was afraid I was going to be sick.

"The waiting is the worst thing of all," Sissy said. "If it wouldn't ruin my makeup, I'd cry."

"I thought you would be used to it by now."

"It gets worse every time," Sissy said.

Frau Dertl came in the dressing room and called me.

"Don't let the older girls get to you, Emmy," she whispered, putting her arm around my shoulders. "The more they perform, the more hysterical they get. You have nothing to worry about. You'll be perfect."

Frau Dertl led the five National Doll dancers and me to the rear of the stage. I heard music and then applause: the end of the first act. We were in the second act.

I went to the hole in the curtain (which stank of old age and dust) and looked for my private audience: My parents, Aunt Anna, Fritz, Marcella, Olaf, and Frau Jensen were in the auditorium. I couldn't find them, but I could see that the auditorium was nearly full. Tickets to the first actual performance were hard to come by, and people called in, or repaid, favors by arranging admission to the dress rehearsal.

Now I was getting really nervous. What if I did something wrong in front of all those people? My hands began to sweat, but I was afraid to dry them on my costume.

Around me, other dancers began to do limbering-up exercises. That was a good idea, I thought; it would keep me from thinking about making a mistake. I limbered up with unusual enthusiasm until Frau Dertl came, wished everyone good luck, and herded us into the wings.

We dipped our slippers into the rosin box and went onto the stage. The first doll box on the left was mine. After I had backed into it, a stagehand handed me the white stiff cardboard lid and I pulled it against the box. It was dark inside with the lid in place.

A moment later I heard the curtain rustle as it went up. Then there was a quick burst of applause.

The music began and I listened carefully

for my cue. I could feel my heart beating. I was scared to death, and wished that I was any place but where I was.

And then I heard my cue!

I pushed the lid forward, and it fell onto the stage. I came out of the box and took three small steps, ending on top of the lid. There was applause. The lights on the stage were so bright after the darkness of the box, that for a moment I couldn't see anything. Frau Dertl had told me to expect the applause and that the orchestra would pause until the applause was over. I was not to move until I had heard my second cue.

When the music resumed, my eyes had adjusted to the bright lights, but I still couldn't see the audience. My legs began to tingle. I took a few more steps to center stage.

Then, to the Johann Strauss waltz, I danced what I had been rehearsing for so long. I knew my legs were going higher than they had when I had practiced with Frau Dertl. And it seemed to me that my position on *pointe* was much more steady than it ever had been.

I felt a little unhappy when I finally had to do my *reverence*. I wanted to keep on dancing.

The music stopped. There was loud applause. All those people were applauding *me*! I was in heaven!

When the applause died and the orchestra started up again, I stepped back into the doll box. The dancer next to me, who represented Hungary, pushed her box lid down and came out of her box. There again was applause.

As the second dancer went through her dance, I thought of Frau Fischer, Herr Strauss, and their two friends, and how all this had begun with my dancing barefoot for them in her music room. Would she have been proud to see me now? I wondered. And then decided she would have been.

After the last dancer had finished and the curtain fell, all of the dolls stepped out of their boxes as the curtain rose again. First, we did a *reverence* together. Then, we each did one separately. We had four curtain calls.

I returned to the makeup room and put the wig back on its plastic head. Then I took off the makeup with glycerine. Frau Hartmann and the other wardrobe mistresses were waiting in the dressing room to help us take off our costumes.

Frau Dertl came, kissed each one of us on the cheek, and said that she was very proud of us to have earned four curtain calls. I thought I could have done better than I had, but decided this was not the time to say so.

My parents, Aunt Anna, Fritz, Marcella, Olaf, and Frau Jensen were waiting for me by the stage door when I came out. My Uncle Otto, who had played in the orchestra, came out, still in his tails, carrying his violin, and congratulated me. My father treated everybody to dinner in a restaurant on Maria-hilferstrasse.

The critics of the next night's performance, identical to the dress rehearsal but before a paying audience, said the *Puppenfee* was "adequate." For the Vienna critics that was the highest kind of praise.

Part Two

Chapter 11

In a very real way, when the final curtain came down on the *Puppenfee*, Act One of my life had come to an end. Although I was still an *élève* and would continue the daily ballet routine, I had inarguably been selected to dance a role in a mainstay of the State Opera's Corps de Ballet's repertoire, and my performance had been judged "adequate" by the critics.

If I was asked to leave the ballet school, it would be because of some misbehavior on my part, not a judgment by Frau Dertl or others on the staff that I didn't have the necessary talent. They went out of their way, of course, to keep my *Puppenfee* role from going to my head, but there was no denying that I had crossed the line between a little girl who dreamed of being a dancer as she might dream of being a bride in a white dress or a princess in a castle, and a girl dancer who with continued training would more than likely become a dancer in the Corps and conceivably even a principal dancer or ballerina.

I had crossed, too, the line between being a little girl and a very young woman. I thought I had found my role in society. When I watched the Corps in training or in a performance, I no longer watched them with the awe of an outsider, but with a professional eye. While I didn't kid myself by thinking that I was as good as the dancers I watched, neither did I kid myself into thinking that I could "never do anything like that." I was convinced that in time, assuming I kept up my training, it was inevitable that I would take my place in the Corps de Ballet as girls like me had earned the right to do for almost two centuries.

What never entered my mind was that the Vienna into which I had been born, the Vienna of the State Opera and the Philharmonic, of the Prater and the Strausses, of flower-decorated *Fiakers*, of coffee topped with whipped cream, of tree-shaded parks and outdoor band concerts, was in its very last days and already had begun to die.

Four months after I danced in the *Puppenfee*, a year after Hitler took over Austria, the German Army, in the pretense that all it was doing was "protecting ethnic Germans from Czech oppression," moved into Czechoslovakia, incorporated the Sudetenland into "Greater Germany" as it had incorporated Austria, and turned the rest of the country into the "Protectorates" of Bohemia and Moravia.

It wasn't much of a war. Some of the Czechs welcomed the Nazis with as much hysterical enthusiasm as the Austrians had, and Great Britian and France ignored the mutual defense treaties they had with Czechoslovakia and let Hitler have his way. The English Prime Minister, Chamberlain, returned from a meeting with Hitler to announce that he was convinced Hitler had no more territorial ambitions and that there would be "peace in our time."

Hitler jubilantly announced in Berlin that he would spend his fiftieth birthday in Vienna. He had been, as an inmate of the Männerheim, at the absolute bottom of Austrian society. Now he was at the absolute peak, the only man in Vienna — for that matter, in the world — who could order a performance of the Vienna State Opera. And he did just that.

The Staatsoper would, the newspapers announced, give a performance of Wagner's *Die Meistersinger*, Hitler's favorite opera, to mark his birthday. It was to be *the* cultural event, and *the* social event, of the year, not only for Austria but for all of "Greater Germany," and for those countries who were either sympathetic to Hitler or afraid to offend him.

The great Birthday Performance day was April 20, 1939. On April 15, when I tried to go to the Opera, I couldn't get across the Ringstrasse. Policemen had put barricades across Ringstrasse, and streetcars were backed up for blocks. Ringstrasse and Kärntnerstrasse to the right of the Opera were jammed with large formations of Hitler Youth and the BDM, many of them carrying flags. They were rehearsing their roles in the ceremonies that would mark Hitler's arrival at the Opera.

It was more than half an hour before they finally all marched off and the police removed the barricades, permitting people to cross the street and the streetcars to move.

I was rarely, almost never, late for my classes and I was afraid of what Frau Dertl would do to me. So far as she was concerned, there was no excuse, not even police barricades, for being late. I ran across the street to the Opera House, now nearly hidden beneath enormous flags and banners.

When I got to the dressing room, however, I found that the other dancers hadn't even started to change.

"What's going on?" I asked.

"Don't you *know*, Emmy?" one of the girls replied. "Haven't you seen the newspaper? It's on the front page!" She handed me the *Kronenzeitung*. A banner headline announced that the Corps de Ballet from the Italian National Opera in Rome would perform in Vienna for Hitler's Birthday Performance.

It was unbelievable. But a moment or two later, Frau Dertl came into the dressing room and confirmed it: She announced that practice was canceled until after Hitler's gala performance. Not only that, we dancers were not to come to the Opera until then, for our rehearsal hall would be in use by the Roman Corps de Ballet. She left quickly, before we could ask any questions.

We never were given any reason for the appearance of the Romans. Some thought it was a political gesture to Benito Mussolini, the leader of the Italian fascists. My father thought it was a studied insult to the Viennese aristocracy, a gesture showing Hitler's contempt for the society in which he had once been a beggar.

"The only thing I know, Emmy," he said sarcastically, "is that your Uncle Otto must be the happiest man in the Opera. He's going to get to play for his beloved leader."

The night of the performance, Uncle Otto did more than play.

When the Vienna Philharmonic began to play the overture of *Die Meistersinger*, Uncle Otto jumped out of his chair, turned toward the swastika-festooned Emperor's box where Hitler and his party were seated, stretched out his arm in the Nazi salute, and bellowed "Heil Hitler!" The other musicians, shocked, stopped playing. The conductor, after an embarrassed pause, rapped his baton on the music stand and started over again.

Our classes at school were now often interrupted by visitors, all women, from Germany. Most of the visiting women wore their hair in braids pinned across the tops of their heads. They spoke a precise, harsh German, and all of them had Nazi brooches, like Frau Müller's, pinned to their dresses.

They all really said the same thing: How happy they were that we had "finally come home to the fatherland" and "how proud we girls must be to be Germans." Soon, we were promised, we "would have the same wonderful life as our brothers and sisters in Germany."

Hearing the same speech over and over quickly bored me. Once, I tried to read a book. The nun who took it away from me was as angry as if she had caught me reading during Mass.

We were required to stand up when visitors entered the classroom, and to wait until they barked "Heil Hitler!" Then we were required to shout "Heil Hitler!" back at them. (Before the *Anschluss*, we had greeted visitors by saying "Grüss Gott.") Marcella and I soon began to bark *"Drei Liter!"* (three quarts), which rhymed with "Heil Hitler." We had heard it somewhere and thought it funny.

One of the Nazi visitors who came to the classroom in a BDM uniform was a much younger woman than the others, and her braids, like mine, hung down below her shoulders instead of being pinned across her head.

In a soft Viennese accent she began her speech by saying how pleased she was to see so many girls in the BDM uniform. Some of the girls in my class wore BDM uniforms. I thought they were much better looking than the school uniform, but had wondered why the teachers said nothing about it; until recently, wearing the school uniform had been required.

When the Viennese visitor said she had come to tell us about the BDM, I was interested. I liked her, and I knew nothing about the BDM except the uniform.

The speaker said that the BDM did many exciting things: They went on weekend camping trips into the mountains and to lakes. Everything — buses, food, and supplies — was furnished free of charge. Athletic instructors offered BDM girls training in a wide variety of sports, from field and track to horseback riding, all at no charge. Some of "our brothers and sisters in Germany," she said, were training for the Olympics.

This was all right down my alley: I loved all kinds of sports. I didn't have any time, of course, because of the ballet, from Monday until Friday, but I thought I could be with the BDM on weekends and during my one month's summer vacation from the Opera.

The BDM, our new visitor said, would take us to Munich to see the Brauhauskeller, a restaurant nearly sacred to the Nazis, where they had met in the early days, and then to Berlin where the leader of the NSDAP (Nazionale Socialistische Deutsche Arbeiter Partei) was now *Führer* of all Germany. If we were lucky, perhaps we might even get to see "Our Leader" in person. She also dangled before us the chance to swim in the North Sea, and even to travel to foreign countries.

I wasn't all that thrilled about seeing Hitler, but the prospect of going to Munich and Berlin was exciting. I had really never been anywhere outside Vienna. When I was little, my father had told me, I had been taken to Prague to see relatives, but I didn't remember that. I also had been to Rome and seen the Pope on his balcony, but I couldn't remember that, either. Now the BDM apparently was going to give me the chance to travel far from Vienna, and free, at that.

The obvious question was asked by a girl wearing the school uniform:

"How can I join the BDM?"

"It's really very easy," the young Viennese visitor replied, holding up a small booklet. "All the details are in this. Take it home and show it to your parents. It will tell you what you want to know about the BDM, and what is expected of your parents." While she passed out copies of the booklet, she went on:

"Our leader, Adolf Hitler, is very proud of his BDM, and he wants his girls to wear their uniforms. In a month, when I return, I'll expect to see *all* of you in uniform." Her face and voice grew solemn: "Remember that the *Führer*'s wish is our command!" She raised her right hand in front of her in the Nazi salute, barked "Heil Hitler!" and left.

As soon as I glanced at the booklet, I saw I had a big problem: There was a photo on the cover of a girl in BDM uniform looking up, almost lovingly, at the swastika in the Nazi flag. There was no question whether or not the BDM was a Nazi organization, and there was no question in my mind about how my parents would feel about that. There would be no joining a Nazi organization, no matter what, or how much, it offered free of charge.

That snap judgment was absolutely correct. When I went home and showed my mother the booklet, her face turned an angry red. "You'll wear a potato sack before you wear a Nazi uniform!" she said flatly. "And don't let your father see that silly book."

That, of course, ended the conversation. There was no point in arguing with her. I took the booklet back from her and hid it between my school books. There must be some way, I thought, I could get around my parents' objections to the BDM. Since all those nice things didn't cost any money, I could say that it was sponsored by the school. Going to Germany, of course, would be more difficult, but maybe Marcella and her mother could help with that.

Stamped inside the cover of the booklet was the information that BDM meetings were held Wednesday evenings at seven o'clock on Mariahilferstrasse. At half past six the next Wednesday I was at Marcella's apartment. I told Marcella not to tell her mother that we were going to the BDM meeting.

"What BDM meeting?" Marcella asked, surprised. "I don't know anything about a BDM meeting. And I don't want to go."

"I want to go," I said.

"I can't believe you!" Marcella said, shocked. "They're all Nazis!"

"I want to go someplace," I replied. I was getting angry. "You go to Sweden all the time. You've even been on an *airplane*. And you go to your grandparents in *Italy*. I haven't been *anywhere*. Not even on a *train*!"

I didn't get anywhere with her. Marcella didn't care about sports, travel, or the BDM, and she flatly announced she would never wear a BDM uniform.

When I left Marcella's apartment, I realized that it was the first time we had ever had an argument like that, with neither one giving in in the end. But then I put Marcella out of my mind.

Chapter 12

When I found the BDM meeting place on Mariahilferstrasse, I recognized the building. It had once been a large antique store, owned by a Jew. The antiques were gone, and the now brightly lit long hall smelled of fresh paint. The old wooden floor in the outer room had been cleaned and varnished. Framed photographs of girls in BDM uniforms hung from the freshly painted walls. There were BDM girls camping, and there were BDM girls walking through fields of flowers. There were BDM girls riding horses and BDM girls running on tracks in a stadium. On the opposite wall were photos of a group of BDM girls looking up at the Eiffel Tower, and of BDM girls on the seashore jumping into the surf. The largest photograph was of Hitler, smiling and shaking hands with one BDM girl while fifty or more BDM girls beamed at them.

A girl in the BDM uniform opened one of the doors in the hall, and I could hear girls' laughter. I asked her where the BDM meeting was. The girl held open the door to the large room in the rear and waved me through it. Inside were round tables and chairs painted in bright colors. It looked like an ice cream parlor.

At the far end of the room was a stage with a row of folding chairs and a wooden lectern. A flag with a huge swastika in the center hung from the wall. I thought it must be the BDM flag, for the swastika was inside a diamond, and a white stripe ran horizontally through the center of the flag. The normal Nazi swastika was in a circle in the center of the flag. Beneath the flag was a large color portrait of Hitler. An upright piano was to the left of the stage.

I didn't recognize anybody and didn't know what to do. Feeling a little uneasy, I stood by the door and waited. A moment later, Lotte Müller, the daughter of the Nazi family who had taken over the Spinats' apartment, ran up to me.

"I'm really glad to see *you* here!" Lotte said. I didn't really like Lotte, and had seldom spoken to her, even at school where we were in the same class. But I was delighted to see her now.

"I'm glad to see you, too, Lotte," I said. "I don't know anybody else."

Lotte led me by the hand to the young Viennese woman who had been at school, and introduced me to Fräulein Catherina Heller. She asked me to sit down at the table where four other girls, none of them in the BDM uniform either, were sitting, and almost immediately clapped her hands to get the attention of the girls in the room.

"I want to introduce the five girls who are going to join us," she said. One by one, she called out names, and motioned for the girl named to stand up. My name was called last.

Led by Fräulein Heller, the BDM girls began to applaud.

I was uncomfortable. Not because of the applause, but because I wasn't at all sure that I wanted to join the BDM. My parents would have a fit if they found out I had even been here. And, except for the ballet, this was the first time that I had ever done anything without Marcella.

I smiled, not knowing what else to do, and told myself that I could always leave if I didn't like what happened next.

When the applause died down, Fräulein Heller looked around the room.

"I see some of you still are not in uniform!" she said. "How do you expect to be in the march if you don't have a uniform?"

One uniformed girl raised her hand, as if in a classroom.

"My mother bought me the uniform," she said nervously, "but she said she couldn't afford buying the shoes."

"Well," Fräulein Heller replied coldly, "just make sure that your shoes are well polished and that you wear white socks."

Then we sang. Song books were distributed, and Fräulein Heller sat down at the piano. She began with *Deutschland über alles*, the German national anthem. Then she played, and the girls loudly sang, a march I had never heard before. The lyrics disturbed me.

"*Es zittern die morschen Knochen der Welt vor dem roten Krieg. Wir werden weiter marschieren, wenn alles in Scherben fällt; die Freiheit stand auf in Deutschland und morgen gehört ihr die Welt.*" (The rotten skeleton of the world trembles before the war of blood. We'll keep marching even when everything falls in shattered pieces. Freedom has arisen in Germany, and tomorrow the whole world belongs to Germany.)

I wondered if the girls really understood the words they were singing.

For half an hour or so the roomful of uniformed, prepubescent girls sang lusty marching songs at the top of their lungs. Afterward, cookies and lemonade were served.

Fräulein Heller took the newcomers aside and told us about the march. The Hitler Jugend (boys) and BDM from all over Vienna would meet in the courtyard of the Hofburg, the Emperor's winter palace, near the Opera, in the Inner Section at two o'clock Sunday afternoon. The Hitler Youth band would provide the music for the march from the Hofburg down the Ring past the Opera to the Stadt Park.

The City Park, the largest park in the Inner Section, has enormous flowerbeds, large tree-shaded paths, and benches surrounding a lake complete with swans and ducks. A band plays Strauss and other Viennese music every afternoon from a bandstand beside an open-air coffeehouse.

Fräulein Heller told the newcomers that we really should have been sworn into the BDM first before being permitted to march, but that since that ceremony took place only on the first Wednesday of each month (last week), as a special favor to us, and provided our parents bought us uniforms in time, we would be permitted to march anyway.

I knew there was no way my parents were going to buy me a uniform right away. Or ever. That meant that I wouldn't be able to march in the parade, and that suited me fine. I needed more time to think this whole BDM thing over. What I wanted from the BDM was a free trip to Munich and Berlin, not the "privilege" of marching down the Ringstrasse in a uniform.

On the way home I told Lotte Müller I didn't think I could make the march.

"My parents can't afford to buy a uniform for me," I said.

"Is that the only reason?" Lotte asked.

I nodded my head sadly, as if shamed, to let Lotte see how sorry I felt for myself because I couldn't be in on the march. I thought my performance was splendid.

"Don't worry about it," Lotte said nonchalantly. "My mother will buy you a uniform!"

I hadn't expected that. It certainly wasn't the same thing as Frau Jensen's buying clothes for me. Frau Müller, a *Nazi*, would buy me a *Nazi* uniform. My mother was going to love that. I had no idea, at the moment, how to handle this unexpected development.

The next day at school, Lotte bought chocolate milk for me at the break. I didn't like that either, and vowed I would buy her milk the next day. Lotte wasn't my friend. But who was? Marcella and I hadn't spoken to each other at school since I had walked out of her apartment. We had been sitting next to each other since first grade, but now I was about to ask the teacher to let me move to another bench. Marcella was making me uncomfortable. I knew that she thought I was a traitor, but as far as I was concerned, Marcella was the one who had betrayed me.

The day after that, as soon as Lotte saw me at school, she cheerfully announced that I should come to the Müller apartment on Saturday morning. Her mother had agreed to buy a BDM uniform for me. I would be able to march in the parade.

Marcella, who overheard the conversation, gave me a look of disgust. I knew that it looked to her not only as if I was going to make friends with Lotte, but that I was joining the Nazi BDM as well.

On Saturday, I told my mother that I was going to Marcella's. That was a safe excuse, for I knew Marcella was mad at me and wouldn't come to my apartment. What did worry me was what I was going to do with the uniform after Frau Müller gave it to me. I certainly couldn't take it home. But I was in too deep to do anything but go down the stairs to the Spinats' — now the Müllers' — apartment.

Frau Müller told me she was happy that I was going to be a BDM, but she didn't say anything about my parents.

The store a few blocks down Gumpendorferstrasse sold nothing but Nazi uniforms, insignia, and other regalia. Glass display cases were filled with the various insignia and on the walls fifty different kinds of Nazi uniforms were displayed.

The saleswoman helped me into a BDM uniform. There was a white cotton short-sleeved blouse, with two breast pockets. The white plastic buttons were stamped "BDM." The skirt, of light black wool, had loops for the official BDM black leather belt and official BDM buckle.

A triangular black scarf went under the collar of the blouse. The ends were held together by a brown, braided leather ring. Finally, there was a black beret. I was shown the proper angle it was to be tilted to the right.

I looked at myself carefully in the mirror and liked what I saw. I looked like the girl on the BDM poster, copies of which had been put up all over the city. And when I walked out of the dressing room Frau Müller and Lotte both said I looked very pretty.

"We'll want the jacket, too," Frau Müller announced. I was delighted. I hadn't expected that. The BDM uniform jacket was a waist-length, brown suede garment with BDM buttons.

Then came the insignia.

From one of the glass cases Frau Müller picked out three identical small porcelain-on-metal insignia. Like the BDM flags, they had a red diamond with a black swastika on a white background. One pin went on the right shirt pocket, the second on the jacket, and the third on the beret.

"Now, let's get her the shoes," Lotte said, ordering the saleswoman around like her mother did.

The whole outfit was topped off with new brown shoes and two pairs of white uniform socks.

While Frau Müller paid for it all, I went back to the dressing room and changed into street clothes.

"Why did you do that?" Lotte asked, following me.

"I don't want to get the uniform dirty before the parade," I lied.

When I came out of the dressing room, Frau Müller said that they had more shopping to do and that I was welcome to join them. I told her I had to go home.

I was afraid to be caught with either Lotte or her mother. If my mother or father saw me with either of them, I would be in trouble. And if my mother or father looked in the bag, I would be doomed. The bag with the BDM uniform in it was a problem anyway. I couldn't bring it into the apartment, I knew that. I thought that if I hadn't been fighting with Marcella I could have left the bag with her. I didn't like the lying, either. My father had told me that you could get away with lying once, but eventually you were inevitably caught at it. I believed him, and I had already lied more than once, and I knew I wasn't through.

When I got to the apartment building, I went down the stairs to the basement. Each apartment had a basement cubicle to store coal. Our bin was the last one on the left side. The BDM uniform and shoes in their paper bag went under the coal.

I felt vaguely guilty, of course, sneaking around behind my parents' backs, but I managed to talk myself out of it: It wasn't my fault; I just wanted to do all those things the other BDM girls did. What was wrong with that?

After lunch on Sunday I told my mother that I was going to the art museum with Marcella and Olaf. She gave me money for a coffeehouse treat afterward. For a moment I felt terribly guilty, but when I thought about putting on my new uniform it quickly passed. I ran downstairs to the cellar, changed into the uniform, and went back up the stairs to the Müllers' apartment to pick up Lotte.

There were boys and girls in Hitler Youth and BDM uniforms on the streetcar to the Inner Section, and when Lotte and I got to the Hofburg, the Plaza outside and the courtyard inside were jammed with several thousand uniformed, excited young Nazis.

The Hitler Youth wore brown shirts, with the same kind of black scarf and leather scarf ring as the BDM. The diamond-shaped insignia worn on their shirt pockets and caps was identical to the BDM pins. The boys wore short black pants, white knee-length stockings, and brown shoes.

It took Lotte and me some time to find our group and Fräulein Heller. And just as soon as we had, a whistle blew and she lined us up in ranks. Each group had a flag, the carrying of which was considered to be an honor. In front of the line of flag bearers was a line of boys, some of whom began making faces at the girls, who, giggling, responded in kind. I was morally outraged. They were behaving like kids, I thought self-righteously, instead of behaving as the serious occasion demanded.

The band began to play music, the command *Vorwärts, Marsch!"* was given, and we marched out of the Hofburg courtyard through the Plaza of Heroes toward the Ring, flags flapping in the breeze.

At the Ring, policemen had stopped both

traffic and the people taking their Sunday strolls. They looked at us curiously. Many smiled, and many even waved.

Ahead of us, boys began to sing. We girls joined in, enthusiastically following Fräulein Heller's instructions to sing as loudly as we could. It quickly became yelling. Over and over I yelled the song I didn't like, the one about the rotten skeleton of the world. But after a while, I stopped singing. I couldn't stand the yelling. I couldn't hear myself singing, or, for that matter, the band playing.

The parade passed the Opera House, and then the Imperial Hotel, where Hitler had stayed, and finally arrived at the City Park.

We were lined up, packed closely together between the flowerbeds, in front of the coffeehouse, and on the dance floor. The Hitler Youth band climbed onto the bandstand. They began to play, and the boys and girls began to sing again. People in the park gathered around, applauding between songs.

I had by now grown bored with the whole affair. I felt like a cow in a herd. I had really felt like a fool marching past the Opera House "singing" at the top of my lungs. Furthermore, my feet hurt. I was tired from marching, and I had a headache from all the noise.

Finally the "singing" stopped, the band left the pavilion, and the groups broke up to go home. I had been separated somehow from Lotte, and to avoid her now I ran to the streetcar stop on the Ring. I didn't feel up to lying to Lotte and I couldn't tell Lotte how disappointed I was with the whole affair. Three girls from my group were already at the streetcar stop. They were obviously delighted with what had happened, and excited by their role in it. Lotte came up and joined us before the streetcar came. She didn't seem to suspect that I had tried to get away from her.

All the way home they talked loudly about what they had done. I was embarrassed because people on the streetcar stared at them. When we finally got to our streetcar stop, I jumped off and ran toward the apartment building. Lotte called for me to wait for her, but I pretended I didn't hear her. All I wanted to do was get out of the uniform as fast as I could. I ran into the cellar and took off the uniform and shoes. When I had my dress on again, I felt an enormous sense of relief. All I had to worry about now was that someone who had seen me wearing it would tell my parents.

The next Wednesday I told Lotte I was sick and couldn't make the BDM meeting. The week after that, I decided the only thing to do was get it over with once and for all. I would just have to tell Lotte the truth: I had had all I could take of the BDM.

"You can't do that, Emmy!" Lotte said, shocked, when I told her I wouldn't be going to the BDM meeting that night. Or again. "You have to go! You're even going to be sworn in."

Marcella overheard the whole thing and gave me an "I told you so" look.

"I'm not going to the meeting," I said. "And I'm *not* going to join the BDM!"

"My mother's not going to like that," Lotte said. When I didn't respond to that, she went on, "My mother will make your mother make you join." I hadn't thought of that possibility. The mental picture of what would happen when Frau Müller told my mother about her ungrateful daughter, who, after she had been *given* a uniform and *marched in the parade*, now refused to join the BDM, was really frightening.

"We'll talk about it later," I said. I had to figure a way out of this new predicament.

When I got to the Opera that afternoon, I was convinced that my sins had already caught up with me.

Frau Dertl came into the dressing room sixty seconds after I had, clapped her hands to get our attention, and demanded:

"Have any of you been approached by the BDM?"

With one or two exceptions, the girls raised their hands.

"And how many of you have joined it?"

Almost half of the class raised their hands. I could see from Frau Dertl's face that she wasn't pleased at all. But at least, I thought, I wasn't going to be alone.

"We don't have time for such things," Frau Dertl went on. "Our work comes first. The government recognizes this. The management will give each of you a letter explaining that you are not to be recruited for the BDM or anything else."

The next day Fräulein Heller came to school. Except for Marcella (exempt because of her father's diplomatic status) and me, everybody was wearing the BDM uniform.

"Where's your uniform, Emmy?" Fräulein Heller asked. "And why haven't you been to the last two meetings?"

"I'm not coming anymore," I replied.

"You're not coming?" Fräulein Heller was angry now; her face had turned red. "You're too busy for the BDM? Is that what you're saying?"

"Yes, that's right," I said.

There was silence in the room as the girls waited to see what would happen to me now.

"Well, we'll see about that!" Fräulein Heller said, raising her voice. "I'll see your parents this afternoon."

"My parents have nothing to do with it," I said quickly. I was no longer afraid of Fräulein Heller. I held out the letter from the Opera. Fräulein Heller snatched it from my hand, opened the envelope, and read the letter.

She didn't like what she read, and she correctly suspected that I was delighted to be in the position I was. But there was nothing Fräulein Heller could do about a decision by the Reichsminister for Propaganda, Dr. Josef Goebbels. Goebbels had decreed that, among other "German" cultural treasures, the Vienna State Opera was considered to be so important to the New Germany that its members were exempt from all Nazi-party-sponsored "Volunteer" activities.

"Emmy," Fraulein Heller announced a moment later to the rest of the class, "has special duties for the State, which will not permit her to be in the BDM, much as we all know she would like to be."

She gave me a frosty smile and handed the letter back to me.

The next day at school Lotte told me that her mother wanted the uniform and shoes back. Before going to the Opera, I ran home and got the paper bag with the uniform, socks, and shoes, and carried it up to the Müllers' apartment. When I rang Lotte's doorbell, Frau Müller answered the door and I handed her the paper bag. She gave me a dirty look and said that the uniform would be given to a girl who really deserved it. Then she slammed the door in my face.

Marcella came to me at school the next day and asked if I wanted to go to the movies on Sunday. I said I did. Marcella didn't mention either the BDM or Lotte to me, and I didn't bring them up either.

Chapter 13

On September 1, 1939, Radio Vienna announced that the German people had been "forced into war with Poland," and that German troops had crossed the Polish border at six that morning.

A new word, *Blitzkrieg* (fast war), came into the language. Within two weeks, Poland had been almost cut in half. On September 17, the Soviet Union, as a result of a secret agreement with the Germans, invaded Poland from the East. The next day, the Polish government fled into Rumania. Warsaw fell on September 28. The last large fragment of the once mighty Polish Army surrendered on October 5. Russia and Germany divided Poland between themselves.

Britain and France finally mobilized their armies, and war was declared.

But that winter, there wasn't much warfare. The real war didn't come until spring. On May 10, 1940, *Blitzkrieg* began in the West.

The Battle of France lasted just about as long as the Battle of Poland. By May 26, the British had begun the evacuation of their soldiers from Dunkirk. On June 10, the Italians did to France what the Russians had done to Poland, declared war on an already beaten country. On June 14, the Germans captured Paris, and an armistice went into effect on June 25.

There were stories in the newspaper, of course, and "Important Announcements" on Radio Vienna. But I had never been to Poland, and I didn't really care when Poland fell to the German Army.

Nor was it really important to me when France, Belgium, and the Netherlands were invaded. All I knew about Paris was that it had the Eiffel Tower and an Opera almost as good as the Vienna Opera. When the newsreel movies showed Hitler in Paris, they showed that the Eiffel Tower and the Paris Opera were undamaged.

I did wonder if Hitler would command the Paris Opera to perform Wagner for him as he had commanded the Vienna Opera to perform *Die Meistersinger*. But when the newspapers reported Hitler was back in Berlin, they said nothing about it.

The first awareness I had that the war was going to affect me was when my cousin, Fritz Schober, showed up at our apartment proudly wearing a *Luftwaffe* (Air Force) uniform with the announcement he had been selected for pilot training.

But at first even seeing Fritz in uniform didn't bring the war close. I was unable to believe that gentle Fritz was *really* going to fly one of the bombers or fighter planes we were always seeing in the newsreels.

Fritz looked very handsome, I thought, in his dark blue Air Force uniform, his cap cocked to the side.

My father got one of his special bottles of wine from the basement and he and Fritz talked about when Fritz was a little boy. Fritz had always loved airplanes. A dozen model airplanes hung from threads in his room.

I was afraid that my father would say something nasty about Hitler and the war, but he didn't. He was very nice to Fritz and cheerful until Fritz had gone. Then my father's face changed. He looked worried.

"I just pray Fritz doesn't get killed," he said. "The poor fool is so young! I didn't have the heart to tell him what I really thought of his becoming a pilot."

"He'll be fine," my mother stopped him. "The war won't last long anyway."

"Let's pray you're right, Olga," my father replied. I could tell he didn't believe her.

Two months after Fritz left for Germany, the war came closer to me again. I had gone to meet Marcella and Olaf at the Baumgarten coffeehouse on the corner of Gumpendorferstrasse and the Ring. Snow had fallen the night before, and on the way I had passed men shoveling snow from the streets. I got to the Baumgarten first and took a table by the window. Olaf and Marcella came in a moment later, red-faced from the cold.

We ordered black coffee with whipped cream and powdered sugar on top, and a butter cream pastry, and sent Olaf to fetch magazines from the racks.

On a kiosk on the sidewalk outside was a recruiting poster. There were recruiting posters all over the city now. This one was of a handsome young man in an Air Force uniform smiling up at an airplane.

"He reminds me of Fritz," I said, pointing at the poster when Olaf returned with the magazines.

Marcella frowned. Olaf ignored me.

Then a moment or two later, Olaf cleared his throat.

"I've got something important to tell you," he said. We looked at him curiously. "I have volunteered for the Army," Olaf announced.

"Olaf, you didn't!" Marcella cried, shocked. Olaf, who had Swedish citizenship, was exempt from conscription.

"I can't stay home when everybody else my age is going," Olaf said quietly.

"What about the Conservatorium?" I asked. Olaf was studying piano at the Horak Conservatory of Music. Olaf loved the piano as much as I loved to dance, and wanted to become a concert pianist. It was not a dream. The Horak Conservatory, which itself was

161

so distinguished that it was known simply as "the Conservatorium," accepted only students of exceptional promise.

"Music will have to wait until the war is over," Olaf replied.

I felt very bad about Olaf's joining the Army. Unlike my cousin Fritz, who was a devout Nazi and believed in what he was doing and loved to fly, Olaf didn't care for the Nazis, and I was sure that deep down he hated war as much as my father.

Marcella and I both realized, however, that it would only make matters worse if we kept on talking about what Olaf shouldn't have done. He had enlisted, and it was too late to talk him out of it.

We gave Olaf a party the day before he left. A small party. Olaf was a loner. He preferred music to just about everything else and didn't have many friends.

Marcella and I baked a cake and prepared open-faced sandwiches. We bought freshly cut flowers from one of the flower stands on Mariahilferstrasse and decorated Olaf's room with them. Marcella talked her mother out of a bottle of champagne she had put away for a special occasion.

Olaf was pleased, but embarrassed. He was always uncomfortable when Marcella and I made a fuss over him. While we nibbled on the sandwiches and sipped on the champagne (which tasted like vinegar to me), Olaf reminded us of the trouble we had given him when we were younger and he had to be our babysitter.

Marcella and I, whenever we could, had been in the habit of ringing apartment house doorbells and then running away, so that when the outraged *Hausbesorger* came out, Olaf was the one who got caught. Once, Olaf recalled, we stole a watermelon at a large vegetable and fruit market in the Fifth Bezirk and we were caught, but Olaf had been forced to pay for the watermelon.

But our worst crime, Olaf recalled, was the tomato juice. Marcella and I, for some unknown reason, had thrown tomato juice out of the Jensens' fourth floor apartment window. What Olaf remembered was that a policeman was walking on the sidewalk below at the time. It had taken all of Olaf's considerable charm to calm down the policeman who came to the apartment with tomato juice soaking into his uniform. It had ended with Olaf solemnly vowing to take better care of his *two* sisters in the future.

I asked Olaf to play for me one last time. He played Chopin waltzes. Olaf had introduced me to Chopin long before Frau Fischer had played it for me on her piano.

Close to tears, I wondered, listening to him play, if as a soldier he would be able to play the piano.

It turned out, at least at first, that he could. When he had been gone about four months, he wrote to me saying that he was in Poland, near the Russian border, and that he had found a job at night playing for his officers in their mess.

After initial successes, which saw the swastika on the outskirts of Moscow and in the rubble of Stalingrad, "General Winter" defeated Hitler's armies as he had Napoleon's more than a century before.

At Stalingrad the Germans suffered their most horrible loss: Over 70,000 men were killed or died of wounds, starvation, or cold, and over 100,000 were imprisoned.

Radio Vienna announced the loss of Von Paulus's Sixth Army at Stalingrad by first playing the second movement of Beethoven's Second Symphony, then announcing the loss, and then reporting that Hitler had declared three days of official national mourning. Theaters and the Opera were closed.

Soon afterward, Propaganda Minister Josef Goebbels announced a "declaration of total war." It was necessary, he said, to make one million more men available for the front lines. Many department stores and restaurants (which had little to offer, in any case) were closed. The places of factory workers drafted into the Army were taken by boys as young as fifteen, men over sixty, and women from seventeen to fifty.

The Vienna Opera, and some theaters and cinemas, Goebbels announced, would remain in operation to provide needed recreation for the people who were now expected to work long hours.

Actually, permitted — even ordered — to function or not, the Opera was most often shut down for lack of coal, and because the technicians necessary to operate it had been drafted for military service or as laborers in factories.

Goebbels, I knew, was a dangerous man. The year before he had ordered that newspapers and tobacco could not be sold to Jews. At the same time, he had forbidden Jews to use public transportation, and Jewish women were forbidden to go to beauty parlors. That was crazy, I thought. What harm could anyone do by using the streetcar or having her hair done? What bothered me most of all, what seemed to prove the Nazis were insane, was the rule that Jews weren't permitted to keep pets. What in the world did a dog, man's best friend, have to do with politics?

After Stalingrad, the German Army was so badly in need of men that even men like my father, who had been exempt from military service because of his "essential work," were ordered into uniform.

My father had talked so much against the war that it had never occurred to me that he would become involved in it. I had always been closer to him than to my mother; he was always there when I needed him, always available to explain whatever puzzled me. I couldn't imagine home without him.

My father reported for basic training, to the Induction Center at the Stiftskaserne on Mariahilferstrasse six blocks from our apartment. I was unable to convince myself that he wasn't really gone, but only around the corner. It seemed to me as if he had gone to the moon.

My mother and I were invited to the Kaserne for the ceremony marking his graduation from his basic training.

We entered the Stiftskaserne (formerly the Royal and Imperial Artillery Academy) through the huge iron gate built for horse-drawn artillery a century before.

Inside was a large, oblong courtyard. On the far side I could see the old stables. My mother and I couldn't find my father at first. It was five minutes before he saw us and came running up to us. He was hardly recognizable in a too-small uniform, which made him look like a boy who had outgrown his clothes. He also walked strangely. Later he told me this was because his boots were too large and he had stuffed them with newspapers to make them fit. I was embarrassed for him.

My father led us to one of many long, wooden benches in a huge hall, and we sat down. With a smile, my father told us he had good news. He had just been told that his request for the ambulance service had been approved.

I felt sorry for my father. He was against the war, but the alternative to service was jail, or worse. I wondered what he would have done if they had forced a rifle into his hands instead of assigning him to drive an ambulance. I knew he couldn't have killed anyone.

When my father and I were alone for a moment, he took my hand.

"It's going to be a bad time, Emmy," he said. "I just wish that you wouldn't have to see it."

All of a sudden he jumped up, clicked his heels together loudly, and stood straight and stiff. I looked at him in alarm. Then my father saluted. An officer came up to us. The officer was a young man whose left arm was gone. An Iron Cross hung around the neck of his well-fitted uniform.

He asked my father to introduce his family to him. The officer smiled at me and shook my mother's hand and told us that he was glad we had been able to come. I watched my father. He didn't move as much as an eyebrow until the officer, saluting again, walked off.

"Do you have to do that all the time?" I asked. I was embarrassed for him again because the officer was so much younger than he was.

"It's part of being a soldier," my father replied.

Loudspeakers blared a command for the men to line up in the front of the hall. My father and a hundred other men in ill-fitting uniforms left their families and lined up as ordered. The stage had a row of chairs; behind them a huge swastika flag had been hung on the wall, over a large, color portrait of Hitler. It reminded me of the stage at the BDM meeting hall.

The graduation ceremony was short. One of the half-dozen officers on the stage went to the microphone and gave a speech. I couldn't understand a word; the microphone made loud crackling noises in the loudspeakers. Then the graduates, in unison, made some sort of reply. I couldn't understand what they said, either. Their voices sounded like thunder and frightened me.

The ceremony was followed by a meal: cold cuts, bread, and ersatz coffee. I looked at all the men with their families and wondered how many of them would soon be killed. Every day the newspapers listed the names of the men who had been killed in action.

My father was given a pass to come home overnight. I was glad that we could get him out of that place and bring him home.

Aunt Anna brought my grandfather and my cousins to our apartment for a little party and dinner. With Grandmother gone, Uncle Otto and Hubert in the Army, and Fritz in the Air Force, it wasn't a very happy family gathering. My father looked disapprovingly at Aunt Anna's Nazi pin, but didn't say anything.

I thought that she knew how my father felt about the Nazis and should have left the pin at home. What made it even worse was that Trudy and Hilde wore their BDM uniforms. I thought that just because my father was in the Army, that didn't make a Nazi out of him. As much as I used to love Aunt Anna, I suddenly disliked her. My grandfather was as kind and almost as cheerful as he used to be before Grandmother died. He made my father laugh and after a few bottles of wine they even began to sing.

The following morning my mother and I took my father to the railroad station. I didn't say good-bye. I just cried. My father had become a soldier and was going off into the war. I knew that since he was in the ambulance service, he would be sent where the fighting was. The enemy was not supposed to shoot at him because he would have a Red Cross painted on his helmet and would wear a Red Cross armband. But what if someone shot him by mistake?

Someone yelled out the order for the men to get on the train. My father kissed my mother and then turned to me. When he kissed me, I saw tears in his eyes. He quickly turned away and got on the train. A few moments later he appeared at an open window. In a hoarse voice, as if something was stuck in his throat, he told us to go home and not to wait until the train left. But my mother and I didn't move. We just stood on the platform and stared wordlessly at him.

A few moments later a whistle blew, and the train slowly began to move. The clacking of the wheels on the train seemed to be saying "Good-bye, good-bye. . . ."

And then I couldn't see my father anymore. Other men waved at my mother and me, and she waved back at them, but I didn't. I was hypnotized by the sound of the train . . . good-bye, good-bye, good-bye.

When the end of the long train had finally left the station and was gone from sight, I had a terrible empty feeling. My father had left me. I didn't know when, or even if, he would ever return. I needed comfort and wanted to go to church. I told my mother and went to the Mariahilfer parish church. I prayed to God as hard as I knew how to please watch over my father and bring him safely home.

The first letter we received from him said that he was in Russia. He was living in the country in a barn, he wrote, but they were on the move constantly and he had hardly any rest. The Germans were fighting the Russians as hard as they could, but weren't successful. It was unbearable, he wrote, having to bury young men who had died before they had had a chance to really live.

After that first letter he never wrote about the war again.

Chapter 14

Vienna changed, became grim, lost its joy.
The streetlights had been turned off. Sandbags blocked entries to buildings and covered
statues in the parks. Windows were either
boarded over or covered with blackout
shades, so it looked as if the buildings had
been deserted. Automobile and truck head-
lights were painted over, except for a tiny
slit. The streetcars, whose windows were
painted over, ran sporadically and sometimes
not at all.

The streets were full of young men in
uniform. Except for the few civilians exempt
from military service because of their jobs,
there were few civilian men who were not
either elderly or Jews. The Jews could be
recognized by the yellow Star of David sewn
onto the breasts of their coats. The Nazis
could be identified by their Nazi buttons.

I had come gradually to understand the
connection between "our glorious victories,"
the daily casualty lists in the newspapers,

and the sad-faced people with black mourning bands on their sleeves.

And then the enemy brought war to Vienna.

Reichsmarschal Hermann Goering, the number-two Nazi, had repeatedly boasted that the German people could call him "Meier" (a common Jewish name) if a bomb was ever dropped on "Greater Germany." After the British bombed Germany in 1940, most people, including some of the Nazis, did. But not in public. Ridiculing public officials was a criminal offense.

There had been rumors that Vienna was going to be bombed, too. My father had told me before he went to Russia that I should expect it would be. After all, he said, the Germans had started the bombing of cities; the enemy had every right to strike back.

The first time Vienna was bombed seemed at first to be nothing more than the nuisance of being awakened at night. There was a Flack (antiaircraft artillery) battery at the Stiftskaserne not far from our apartment, and the cannon made a lot of noise when they fired. But the bright white flashes of the Flack exploding in the sky, like firecrackers, was fascinating, even beautiful. I jokingly told my mother that our studio apartment windows gave us the best seat in the house.

I stopped joking the next day when I saw that several of the magnificent buildings along Ringstrasse had been bombed into rubble. And I was ashamed that afternoon when the newspaper carried the names of those killed, including many children.

The park two blocks from our apartment, where I so often had gone with Petja, lost its trees and flowerbeds. They were cut down and torn out so that a big, ugly, gray windowless concrete bunker could be built. When the horribly shrill whine of the sirens started, hysterically screaming women, dragging whimpering children behind them, ran from all directions to the bunker's air raid shelter. I was as afraid of being crowded into the shelter with so many people, many of them crazed, as I was of the bombers. After the first air raid, I never went back to the bunker.

I went instead into the basement of our apartment building. Behind the coal bins was a very large room used to store excess furniture. We moved the furniture out and made a place for cots with blankets and pillows, comfortable lounging chairs, and small tables.

From narrow windows close to the ceiling I could see the feet and ankles of people passing by on the sidewalk.

Most air raids were at night, and my mother always kept a suitcase packed with extra clothes, medicine, our important papers, candles, matches, playing cards, books, and food to take with us into the shelter.

One night during a raid, Frau Müller suddenly screamed: "Someone stole my cookies!"

Petja was the thief. He came out from underneath Frau Müller's cot and licked his tongue. Everybody but Frau Müller thought it was funny and laughed. She picked up the plate. A few cookies remained. She handed it to me.

"I won't eat these," she announced, "after that animal had his mouth on them."

My mother and I ate the rest of the cookies. They were delicious, made out of white flour, sugar, eggs, and butter. The next day my mother was sternly warned by the authorities about the penalties for bringing a dog into a shelter. There was no question in my mind who had told the authorities about Petja.

When there was an air raid during the day-time, I always tried to make it home to our cellar. There were persistent rumors that some people didn't permit strangers to seek shelter in their cellars, and I was terrified of being caught on the street with nowhere to go. Marcella shared my fear, and on Satur-days we always ran as fast as we could to get to the other's apartment, and took pains to be sure it would still be light when we went home.

One Saturday, half a dozen blocks before I reached Marcella's apartment, the sirens went off. Almost immediately, I heard the boom-ing of the antiaircraft cannon, which meant that the air raid warning had been given too late.

People began to run for shelter. I tried to decide whether to run to Marcella's house or to mine. I was scared sick to realize that with the antiaircraft cannon firing already steadily that it was too late to run either way. Except for one man, I was the only person left on the street.

"Get into a shelter!" he screamed at me, and then ran off.

I ran into the next apartment doorway. The steel door to the cellar shelter was locked. I banged on it with my fists. After a moment, a woman inside called out to ask who was there and I called out my name. The woman shouted that the shelter was full and told me to try some place else.

Literally shaking with fear and chilled by a clammy sweat, I went back out onto the street. The antiaircraft cannon were firing steadily and I heard and felt the thundering explosions of bombs landing not far away. I ran to the next apartment building, praying that the people there would let me into their cellar.

An elderly, white-haired, gentle-looking man opened the shelter door, smiled at me, and motioned me inside. He led me to a straight-backed wooden chair with a cushion on it. He introduced me to his wife, and told me that if I wanted something just to tell his wife.

"She'll take good care of you," he said.

I began to cry, either because the people in the first shelter had been so cruelly selfish or because the elderly couple here were so kind and generous, or both.

I looked around the shelter. It wasn't as

large as ours, but it was as cold and damp, and I shivered. I counted thirteen people. Except for the man, the others were all women and children: three elderly women, four young women, and five preschool children. The older children sat on an old rug and played with their toys. Two very small children were asleep. They didn't understand what was going on and had no fear.

Even in the shelter I could hear the booming of the antiaircraft and the thunder of exploding bombs. It seemed both as if there was much more noise than earlier, and that it was coming closer and closer.

Suddenly there was a strange swishing, sucking sound, followed by a terrible, loud roar. The walls rocked and the floor shook under my feet. I heard something falling onto the ceiling of the shelter and then the other side of the walls.

The shelter door burst open and rubble poured down the stairs. The young women began to scream, and all the children (including the little ones who had been asleep and had been awakened) began to howl in fear.

The wall behind me cracked open with a tearing sound and rubble poured through a jagged opening. There was no question now — the building had been hit.

Before I had a chance to accept this, one of the young mothers became hysterical. She screamed and literally started to pull her long, red hair from her head. The crazed look on her face frightened me even more.

The old man who had let me into the shelter left his wife, who was sitting next to me, and went to the woman. He grabbed her shirtfront with one hand and slapped her, hard, on the face with the other. She stopped screaming instantly. She looked at him a moment and then she picked up the youngest of her children and began to comfort her. When the child stopped crying, she knelt and began to comfort the other child.

The old man returned to his wife and put his hand on her shoulder. "I'm sorry," he said, ashamed that he had hit a woman. His wife gently patted his hand, telling him she understood; it was all right.

Parts of the building continued to fall. The stairs, the only way out of the cellar, were now completely blocked. The terrible noise of a few minutes before gave way to a silence that was just as frightening.

The old man went to the center of the room and quietly reassured everyone. The worst was over, he said. All that was needed now was patience to wait until the air raid was over and people could begin to get us out.

One of the young women asked him what would happen if they couldn't find us. He told her confidently that she need not worry, we would be helped.

Time passed very slowly. An hour after we were hit, the faint noise of a siren announced that the air raid was over. Everyone listened intently for the sounds that would mean someone was trying to rescue us. But there was nothing.

The children, exhausted by the excitement, eventually went to sleep on the rug. The young mothers huddled together, whispering.

For two hours there was no sound from the outside world. I wondered what would happen if the old man was wrong. What if we couldn't be rescued in time? Would we suffocate from lack of oxygen?

There was another groaning, cracking noise. Still more rubble spilled into the basement, and water began to drip and then to gush through the jagged, bulging crack in the wall. The elderly woman took me over to the other side of the room. As the water moved toward the rug, the young women picked up their children and held them on their laps. We tried to convince ourselves that the reason for the rubble and the water was that rescue workers were trying to work themselves down to us.

The young women started to feed their children. The elderly woman saw me watching them hungrily, touched my arm, and handed me a sandwich. It was good rye bread spread with a thin layer of lard. I thanked her.

Four hours after we were hit, there were muted but unmistakable sounds of banging and voices.

"We're here! We're here!" everyone screamed.

The sounds became louder and louder. And then we could make out someone yelling: "We're coming! We're coming!"

Crying with relief, everyone in the shelter hugged each other.

It was more than an hour before a face appeared in the rubble at the shelter door. I kissed the obviously exhausted rescuer, who took my hand to lead me out of what almost had been my tomb.

The street outside was blocked with the remains of the building I had been in, and the streets on my way home were blocked with piles of rubble that hours before had been someone's home.

My mother was less disturbed by what had happened to me than I thought she would be, but it gave her the opportunity to bring up something she had had on her mind. She was afraid for my safety and didn't want me to go to the Opera anymore.

Some of the girls in the ballet had stopped coming already, but they lived much farther away than I did. But I wouldn't tell my mother that. I needed my other, my happy world, and couldn't imagine life without the Opera ballet. My mother tried very hard to convince me that I should stay home, but I began to cry and she finally gave in.

I was spending more and more time at the Opera. In addition to the ballet classes, I had begun (because no other children or young people were available) to take part in some of the operas, as an extra. All of us felt privileged to be asked to be on stage even if no dancing was involved.

The Corps de Ballet, furthermore, was now offering an every-other-week performance for wounded soldiers. I was permitted to dance regularly in that. With my hair pulled tight in the back in a bun, and wearing a gold-embroidered white tutu, I had a solo on *pointe*, and danced to a Chopin waltz.

When my picture had been in the newspapers with the story of the first performance for the wounded, I bought enough copies to send my father, Fritz, and Olaf each a copy of the clipping.

There was little else offered in the way of entertainment in Vienna, and the Opera was generally packed for our performances. I learned that I could count on more applause from the soldiers than I had received from any other audience.

But when I looked through the hole in the curtain and saw so many young men with white bandages on their heads, arms, or legs, or missing arms and legs, some of them even sitting up on stretchers in the aisles, I felt very sad.

My outlook toward performing had changed since I danced in the *Puppenfee*. I had then been so excited I thought of nothing else but being on stage. Now the excitement of being on stage was still there but was overwhelmed by concern that I was not going to be as good as I could be, or worse, that I would make a terrible mistake.

Sometimes when I stood behind the stage waiting for my cue, I could feel my heart beating and was so afraid that I didn't want to perform at all. But when I got the cue to go before the brilliant footlights a strange thing happened: I wasn't afraid. When I heard the familiar music, I went into another world.

It was a better world, that make-believe world on the stage, than the real one outside.

Chapter 15

One afternoon a week before Christmas 1943 Marcella and I went window shopping on Mariahilferstrasse. We couldn't go at night because neither the streets nor the windows were lit. The streets were packed with snow, and I remembered how beautiful Mariahilferstrasse had been at night before the war with the lights from the decorated windows reflecting on the snow.

Marcella and I had been best friends since the first grade. But we had grown even closer to each other as a result of our personal problems. Marcella had lost her father as her confidant when he moved out of their apartment and in with his mistress. And when Olaf went into the Army, she lost him. After my father went off to the Army, Marcella and I had only each other.

As the Christmas holidays approached, we felt even more alone.

I thought it was foolish to "celebrate." There was very little to celebrate. There wasn't enough coal to keep warm, or enough food to eat. Food was closely rationed. It seemed grossly unfair that before the war my parents didn't have the money to buy me presents, and now that we had money there was hardly anything to buy.

There were three categories of food ration coupons: "Light Workers" (including house-wives and children), "Medium Workers" (office workers), and "Heavy Workers" (manual laborers).

Medium Workers received a slightly larger food ration than Light Workers, and Heavy Workers received about twice as large a ration as Medium Workers.

All members of the Corps de Ballet received Heavy Workers food rations. The ballet had been officially determined to be "heavy work, in support of the war effort."

But having ration coupons did not automatically mean that you got the food to which you were officially entitled. Everything was in short supply, and stores quickly sold out of whatever food they received. The result was long lines of housewives and children before all food stores.

People in the lines who knew my mother and me and knew we didn't work in a factory and who saw that we had Heavy Workers ration coupons didn't like it. They knew that Heavy Workers coupons were available on the Black Market. They were very expensive and bought mostly by big-shot Nazis. They presumed we had gotten ours that way.

At first, I explained that we had the Heavy Workers coupons because I was in the Corps de Ballet. The reaction to this was snickers, and some people called my mother a traitor and me a little Nazi. I gave up trying to explain and just ignored the jibes and dirty looks.

Not only food was rationed. There were coupons for clothes and shoes, too. Children and young people whose feet were still growing were hurt the most by the leather shortage. When I outgrew my shoes, new leather shoes were simply not available.

The ration was two pairs of wooden-soled shoes a year. The soles were made of three separate pieces of wood. When the flesh of the foot, especially the ball, got between the pieces, they pinched painfully. I tried to solve that problem by bandaging my feet and then putting heavy woolen stockings over the bandages. If I didn't stay out too long in the snow or rain, the bandage helped protect my feet, too. But in the summer the bandages made my feet sweat badly, gave them blisters, and made them look ugly.

My mother, of course, and other adults could still wear their old leather shoes. She would have given me her shoes, but my feet were already two sizes larger than hers. When it was wet, my mother stood in the food lines for me.

The young had the same kind of problem with clothing. The adults had their prewar clothes, but when children outgrew their clothes, what was available on the ration was of very poor quality. When the winter coat I got on my ration was much too thin for the cold weather, my mother made a coat from a heavy, bright plaid blanket for me.

Marcella was just about in the same boat. Her father, who wasn't as big a man as my father, gave her his winter coat. Frau Jensen had shortened it, but it was too large in the shoulders for her. We looked like clowns in a third-rate circus. But we were warm, and that was all that mattered.

As we window-shopped along Mariahilferstrasse, Marcella suddenly stopped me and pointed to the display window of a pastry shop. I couldn't believe my eyes: Not only was it open (most of them had been closed for some time because of the shortage of sugar, eggs, butter, and milk and because the only available flour was dark gray), but the window offered a display of delicious-looking, pink and yellow pastries.

There were no other customers in the shop and I wondered why. I hadn't seen real pastry on sale for a long time. We hurried inside. A gray-haired waitress in a black dress, wearing a small white apron around her waist and a stiff, white lace band in her hair, stood behind the counter.

Afraid to believe our good luck, we asked her how many ration coupons were required for a piece of the pastry. We always carried coupons and money, hoping to come across a sign in front of a coffeehouse or restaurant announcing a special treat for so many coupons. And, because we were always hungry, our mothers saw to it that we had some of their "extra" coupons.

Looking somewhat embarrassed, the waitress said we didn't need any coupons. We ordered the pastry. When it was served, the waitress apologized that she couldn't offer us anything but water to drink. We didn't mind. All we wanted was a sweet piece of real pastry.

I took a healthy bite. My mouth puckered up inside. The pastry tasted like soapy sawdust. I looked at Marcella. She couldn't keep the dainty bite of pastry she had taken in her mouth. She spit it out and quickly gulped down some of the water. I had swallowed mine and was afraid I was going to throw up.

After a moment, Marcella began to laugh and pointed at me. "You should see yourself," she said. "You look as if you've swallowed a rat!"

"Now we know why nobody is in here," I said.

The waitress came to the table and quickly took the plates away.

"You don't have to pay for that," she said. "I shouldn't have served you that sawdust in the first place, but I was told to."

She seemed so ashamed that Marcella and I felt almost as sorry for her as we did for ourselves, but when we were out on the street we started to laugh again at our own stupidity. There was no real pastry in Vienna, and we should have known it.

People on Mariahilferstrasse looked at us curiously. There was very little laughter on the streets in those days. When we passed the shop again on our way home, there was a "Closed" sign in the window and the delicious-looking "pastries" in the window were gone.

While everything else comfortable and familiar in Vienna seemed to be closed, or drastically changed, the Opera remained open and functioning. Opera-loving Viennese sat uncomplaining in the unheated building, and didn't even seem to mind when the performances were regularly interrupted by air raids and everybody ended up in cellars. Programs included instructions about what to do during an air raid.

Propaganda Minister Josef Goebbels, who had insisted that the Opera remain open because of the morale contribution it made to "Total War," changed his mind in the spring of 1944. The war was going badly for Germany, and the war machine could no longer afford something as totally unwarlike as the Opera. Goebbels drafted the artistic world into his Total War. The Opera's technicians, and even some singers and dancers, were put in uniform, and the building itself was ordered closed until "Final Victory."

It meant the end of the Corps de Ballet, and of the Ballet School, too. When Frau

Dertl announced that our classes were being suspended until the war was over, I cried. The ballet was the only happy world I had.

"But there is some good news," Frau Dertl continued. "I've arranged for all of you to be accepted at the Conservatorium. They've promised to turn one of their rehearsal halls over to us, and we can continue practice there."

The sense of relief that I felt when I heard that I could continue my study vanished when I had a chance to think it over a moment. The Horak Conservatory, unlike the Opera, was a private institution. Frau Dertl's ability to have us accepted there, en masse, wasn't going to do me any good because I couldn't afford the tuition, no matter what it was. My father was only a private, and the soldier's allotment my mother received hardly covered our rent and food. Now I was really unhappy.

But Frau Dertl came through for me, and other girls who were in the same financial boat as I was. She kept about a dozen of us behind:

"I know that most of your parents can't afford the Conservatorium fees," she said. "But I think I've found a way to get around that."

There were sighs of relief.

"I've gotten in contact with some old friends of mine, of the Ballet's, at Rosen-hügel," she continued. "They understand the problem, and are going to do what they can to help."

Rosenhügel was Vienna's Hollywood, our movie studios. I wondered how they could help. I had heard why they had been permitted to remain in operation. The official reason was the same one Goebbels had used for keeping the Opera functioning as long as it had, their contribution to morale, and thus the war effort. The real reason was that Nazis owned substantial interests in Rosenhügel. They had "bought out" the Jews who had owned much of the Austrian (and German) motion picture industry before the Nazis. And motion pictures, since there was no other entertainment, were now making them enormous sums of money.

"What they're going to do is get you a day or two's work a week. Most of the time you'll be extras. There are a few dancing roles — not ballet, but dancing — and when they come up, you'll be given first try for them. There may even be some speaking parts, though I wouldn't count on getting them. But the money's good, and one day's pay will take care of your tuition at the Conservatorium."

Again, I was momentarily delighted with Frau Dertl's announcement. The idea of being in the movies was, of course, exciting, and if it would also provide the money for my Conservatorium tuition, my problems seemed to be over. I had a couple of delightful moments to wonder how I was going to look on the silver screen as a rich and famous movie star, and then I crashed down to reality again.

What was I going to do about school? I might get away with playing hooky one day now and then, but there was no way I could get away with regularly cutting a day or two every week. I needed my father now, I thought. I could explain to him why it was more important for me to go into the movies instead of to high school, but I was not going to be able to convince my mother of anything like that. And if she wouldn't let me go to the movie studio, I couldn't continue studying ballet with Frau Dertl. I felt like crying again.

But she surprised me. When I told her about what Frau Dertl had arranged for us and how I really had to drop out of school, I didn't even get an argument. If going to the movie studio would make me happy, it would be all right with her. It wasn't as if I wanted to get out of working. Going to the studios at Rosenhügel, and then going to ballet class, would be much harder than going to school had been. For the first time I felt as close to her as I had to my father.

The following Friday I received a postcard ordering me to report for work at Rosenhügel, the movie studio, at six o'clock the following Monday morning. My mother said that she would call the school and tell them I was ill, and that I would be out for a day or two.

Although I could hardly wait to tell Marcella about my new life as a movie star, the next morning, I waited until the mailman came at eleven o'clock before leaving for her apartment. Neither Marcella nor I had heard from Olaf for quite some time, and if there was a letter, I wanted to take it with me. But the mailman didn't knock on our door.

I decided that I would make some excuse for being so late in going to her, rather than mention the mail.

Marcella, especially when I was late, usually looked out the window to wait for me, and then would be waiting by her open door for me when I got to the apartment. But that morning she wasn't waiting for me, and I had to ring the bell. When Maria, the maid, opened the door, her face was gray white.

"What's wrong, Maria? Are you sick?" I asked. She started to say something, but instead burst into tears. "Where's Marcella?" I asked.

Maria, sobbing, pointed with her hand and arm toward the living room. I sensed that something was dreadfully wrong, but I didn't want to think what it most probably was.

When I went into the living room, Marcella was sitting on the couch between her parents. The three of them looked at me almost without recognition. The looks on their faces frightened me.

Herr Jensen's presence convinced me that something had happened to Olaf. Otherwise, he would not be there. Since he had moved in with his mistress, he seldom came to their apartment. He took my hand and led me to Marcella. I was afraid to say anything, so I just sat down next to her.

Herr Jensen walked over to the window. Frau Jensen got up and followed him. And then, suddenly, Marcella threw her arms around me.

"Olaf is dead!" she sobbed, confirming my worst fears. I had desperately hoped that he had been wounded, or captured. I didn't want to believe what I had heard.

"He was moved to the Russian front," Marcella's father said quietly, without turning his head from the window and as if that explained everything.

I held Marcella's face against my chest and cried, too. After a while Marcella stopped weeping, sat up, took a handkerchief out of her pocket, and blew her nose.

"What happened?" I asked.

"I don't know," Marcella mumbled. "An officer went to the Embassy this morning and told Daddy that Olaf had been killed in action."

"Maybe they made a mistake," I said, trying to find hope somewhere.

Marcella didn't reply. She began to cry quietly.

The front doorbell rang and a moment later Dr. Hoffman, Herr Jensen's best friend, came into the living room. I knew him well and liked him. Often, when I had gone with Marcella and Olaf to see their father, he had taken all of us to the Prater and later to a restaurant, and Dr. Hoffman had frequently joined us. Marcella and Olaf had known him since they were little; they called him Uncle Hans.

"I was in the operating room all morning," he said apologetically. "I came as soon as I could."

Herr Jensen shook hands with him, but Frau Jensen didn't leave the window. Dr. Hoffman went to Frau Jensen, kissed her, smiled sadly at me, and then went to Marcella. He sat down next to her and took her into his arms.

"I want to die, Uncle Hans," she moaned.

"Don't say that," Dr. Hoffman said. "Olaf wouldn't want you to talk like that." He lifted her chin and made her look into his eyes. "We can't change anything. Olaf is in God's hands now."

I wished that he hadn't said that about God. Why did God let Olaf get killed? Olaf had never hurt anybody in his life. He wasn't even a Nazi!

I got up and went into Olaf's room. Max, his beige and black shepherd dog, was in there. Since Olaf had gone, Max hardly ever left Olaf's room. I lay down on the floor beside large, gentle Max, patted him, and began to cry. He licked my cheek. I knew how much Max missed Olaf, how he waited for him in his room. And now Olaf would never return.

I heard Dr. Hoffman tell Frau Jensen to take the pills he had given her and to go to bed. And then he came into Olaf's room.

"Come on, Emmy," he said, helping me to my feet. "Let's put Marcella to bed. Right now, that's the best thing for her." He put his arm around my shoulders and walked slowly back into the living room with me.

Marcella at first refused to take the pills Dr. Hoffman gave her and said she didn't want to go to bed either. But eventually she gave in, and Dr. Hoffman led her to her room, closing the door behind them.

Herr Jensen told me there was nothing he and I could do anymore and that he would take me home. He would stay the night, he said, and he asked me to come back in the morning. When Marcella woke up, he said, she would need me.

My mother wasn't home when I got there. I found one of Olaf's letters:

Dear Emmy,

I am a little homesick and wish that I could take you and Marcella to a coffeehouse for coffee with whipped cream and a piece of cake.

Last night I played Chopin waltzes for a general. He liked Chopin almost as much as you do.

In your last letter you mentioned that you are sometimes tired of going to your daily ballet lessons. You don't know how lucky you are! I miss the Conservatorium very much and wish I could practice until my fingers hurt.

Write soon again, please.

Olaf

I read his letter over and over again, and began to cry. I cried for a long time.

While I was having breakfast, Marcella called. Her voice sounded strangely calm. I realized it was the pills Dr. Hoffman had given her. Her mother, Marcella said, was taking her to Italy to be with her mother's parents. She said she didn't know when she would be back.

I wondered about Olaf's funeral, but was afraid to ask.

"If you want to know about the funeral," Marcella said, reading my mind, "forget about it. There won't be a funeral." I thought I had misunderstood her and waited for her to go on, but Marcella didn't say anything else. There was a somehow frightening silence over the telephone.

After a long pause, I asked, "Are you still there?"

"I'm still here," Marcella replied emotionlessly. "We can't bury Olaf. We don't have his body. The Army had to retreat suddenly. They left the wounded and dead behind."

"What are you going to do?" I asked, horrified.

"I'm going to Italy to see my grandparents," Marcella repeated, in the same frightening, toneless, calm voice. "There'll be a Memorial Service for him at the Embassy. I don't know when. I have to go, Emmy. I'll call you when I come back."

Marcella hung up before I had a chance

to say good-bye to her. I looked out the window. The sun was out, and the clouds were white. Olaf was behind a cloud, and he was safe now, I thought. Then I said The Lord's Prayer.

Chapter 16

I never got to tell Marcella that I was going to be in the movies. And I never would have the chance to tell Olaf.

But at five o'clock the next morning, when it was still dark, I got onto a dark, cold streetcar for the trip to Rosenhügel. It had been no more than a thirty-minute ride before the war, but now it would take over an hour.

The people on the streetcar depressed me. Aside from a few elderly men, most of the passengers were gray-faced women on their way to work in factories. They were dressed in wornout, dirty looking clothing, their hair was uncombed, and many of them had their eyes closed and seemed to be asleep. Others just stared at the floor. They were, I realized, little more than human extensions of the machines they operated.

They had lost hope, given up, and that struck me as strange because the streetcar also carried two women who had Stars of David pinned to their coats. Sometimes, if a

Jew was married to a Christian, he or she managed to escape, at least for a time, being sent to a concentration camp. Instead, they had to do manual labor in factories. If anyone should have given up hope, I thought, it should be the Jews, but these women didn't seem to have given up. Their clothing was clean and neatly patched, and, most significantly, their hair was neatly fixed.

I felt like an intruder looking at them and was glad when all of them got off the streetcar and walked toward the entrance of a big factory.

It was just getting light when I finally arrived at Rosenhügel's large main gate. I showed an elderly uniformed guard the postcard I had been sent. He pointed his often-mended glove, singling out one of many one-floor, gray, concrete-block buildings.

"Building C," he said, opened the gate, and tipped his hat. Nobody had ever before tipped his hat to me. I happily decided he thought that I was an actress, and someone special, and that was enough for me to put the unpleasant memory of the sad women on the streetcar — Jew and "Aryan" — from my mind.

Building C turned out to be an office building with a sign reading "Admittance." Inside was a door with a "Report Here" sign on it. A heavy-set woman in her late fifties sat behind a small desk. I saw half a dozen of my friends from the Opera, including one boy, sitting on wooden chairs against the wall. They smiled at me, and I saw they were as nervously excited as I was.

There were the inevitable forms to be filled out, and then the stout woman led us out of a rear door of Building C to another of the one-story concrete-block buildings. As we followed her, I had the nasty thought that we looked like six muddy piglets following their mother. As we approached the building I saw a sign reading "Wardrobe & Makeup." Then the door opened and an immaculately made-up young woman purposefully strode out. She was wearing a white blouse, riding boots, and breeches. She had a fur coat over her shoulders.

She looked quickly and disdainfully at us, and then dismissed us as unimportant. It took me a moment to realize that what we had seen was not a young woman off at a very early hour for a ride on a horse, but an actress (the makeup proved that) on her way to work. A moment after that, I realized that the actress was familiar. I had, I decided, seen her in the movies.

The Wardrobe Department, with its long rows of benches and clothing hooks on the walls, and wardrobe mistresses bustling busily around, looked very much like the wardrobe rooms at the Opera. I found this comforting, and told myself that I wasn't a complete novice, theatrically speaking. I was a little surprised to see that many of the women changing into long and wide dresses looked fifty or sixty years old, and then professionally decided that a good makeup man could make an old woman look like a girl.

One of the wardrobe mistresses gave me three ruffled petticoats to put on, and then helped me into a lace-trimmed pink floor-length dress. She told me that we were lucky: "Director Willy Forst's movie is right down your alley."

"What's it about?" I asked.

"It's called *The Viennese Girls*," she said. "It's set in the time of Empress Elizabeth."

After we were dressed, we went to Makeup. The makeup man painted my face as carefully, but not quite so garishly, as the makeup men in the Opera had. Then he took a natural-looking wig from its storage head and carefully arranged its long, Baroque-era curls over my own hair.

When I examined myself in the mirror, I was surprised at how natural I looked. Made up for the stage of the Opera, I had looked unnatural. The lighting for movies, I decided, must be different than the stage lighting at the Opera.

Seeing myself made up made me think of the actress in the riding habit I'd seen as we came toward the building.

Then, all of a sudden, I knew where I had seen the actress before. It hadn't been on the movie screen, but at the Opera. The first time I'd seen her was on the day of my audition, when, dressed in a tutu, she had looked down her nose at me because I was wearing my confirmation dress. The last time I had seen her was the day she had quit. The actress I had seen was Ilse.

"Do you know an actress named Ilse Novak?" I asked the makeup man.

"I know her," he said without emotion.

"So do I," I bubbled, and then boasted: "We're old and very dear friends."

That didn't get the response I expected. He raised his eyebrows in surprise, but it wasn't a pleased surprise. I had said something wrong. I didn't know what, but I knew enough to let the matter drop right there.

Franz, the only boy in our group, came into the makeup room dressed in a dark blue velvet suit with a white ruffled shirt. He looked far more handsome in the Belle Epoque costume than he did in his regular clothes.

When the makeup men had finished with all of us, the stout woman, sharply ordering the girls to lift our dresses so they wouldn't drag on the ground, herded us to a large, tall, warehouselike building identified by a sign as "Studio Four." Inside was a long, gray, cement-floored hall. Four steel doors opened off it. Above each door was a large light fixture with a red globe. On each door was a warning: DO NOT ENTER WHEN LIGHT IS FLASHING.

Only one red warning light was flashing, but three of the doors were closed. The fourth was open, and I could hear a lot of noise inside as a stream of people walked in and out of it.

The stout woman brusquely ordered us to

be quiet and then led us inside, where it was so brightly lit that it took a moment for my eyes to adjust. Then I saw the set. It was an old-fashioned drawing room furnished with lovely antique furniture. There were Oriental rugs on the floor, and paintings and candelabra on the walls. Floodlights and spotlights were mounted on scaffolding overlooking the set where the ceiling of a real room would be.

There were men in gray coveralls on the scaffolds and on the set itself two set dressers were hanging a large painting on the wall at the direction of a man in a tweed sports coat. The painting showed a pretty young woman in a beautiful long, wide Baroque gown covered with lace and jewels. I recognized her as Empress Elizabeth.

Off to one side of the set were two large motion picture cameras with a dozen people clustered around them. Two men were sitting in folding canvas chairs close to the cameras.

The stout woman went to one of the men in the canvas chairs and said something to him. He turned around, looked at us, and then got up and walked over to us. I had recognized him right away: He was Willy Forst, the well-known Austrian movie director.

"So," he said, smiling, "you are Frau Dertl's students. I'm sorry that we don't have any dancing parts for you right now. But we'll find something for you to do, as extras, or maybe even little roles where you say a word or two."

I was impressed. I was going to be an actress. Why not? Ilse was an actress. I had been a better dancer than she was, so clearly I could be a better actress. How exciting!

"But since you are dancers," Herr Forst continued, "and dancing roles pay better than extras, we'll consider whatever you do dancing."

He turned and walked back to his folding canvas chair. I saw that his name had been painted on the canvas back. Then I recognized the man sitting in the chair beside him, confirming my identification by reading what had been painted on his chair: Paul Hörbiger.

Hörbiger was a legitimate Austrian (now German) movie star. I had seen him fifty times on the screen. He was in costume, one much like Franz's except his was black.

A half an hour or so later, Herr Forst returned to us. He looked us over and selected three of the girls, one at a time, by pointing his finger at them. I was crushed. He hadn't pointed at me. He motioned for the three girls he had selected to follow him onto the set, where he positioned them on the couch and on upholstered chairs. Then he pointed his finger at Franz and me and gestured for us to come onto the set.

"All of you are Herr Hörbiger's children," he said, loudly enough for everyone to hear. "And you two," he said, pointing at

Franz and me, "are going to be asked by your father why you haven't practiced the piano."

I was going to get a speaking role. My motion picture career was off to a flying start!

Director Forst looked at Franz: "You answer, 'Because I didn't feel like it, Father.' All right?" Then he turned to me and gave me my very first lines: "Because I didn't feel like it, either."

"Can you do that, *Liebchen?*" he asked.

"I think so," I said modestly. What a silly question! He wasn't dealing with some rank beginner. He was dealing with me, whose performance as the Austrian Doll in the *Puppenfee* had been judged "adequate."

I told myself that it was about time I had some good luck, and now I was going to have it. My first role would be opposite *Paul Hörbiger.* I wondered if my name would appear on the advertising posters.

Herr Forst put Franz and me in front of Hörbiger, and then quickly left the set. Hörbiger smiled at us graciously.

"Test, please," a man shouted. The murmurs and talking and sounds of equipment being moved around stopped.

"Action!" Willy Forst called out.

Paul Hörbiger turned to Franz and sternly demanded, "Why haven't you practiced the piano?"

"Because I didn't feel like it, Father," Franz replied quickly and smoothly.

Paul Hörbiger turned to me. "And why haven't you practiced the piano?"

I opened my mouth to say, "Because I didn't feel like it, either." I got as far as "Because" and then broke into embarrassed, uncontrollable giggles.

Paul Hörbiger gave his costar a look of mingled amusement and annoyance.

"Cut!" a man shouted. People began to move around and talk to each other again.

Willy Forst waved me over to his director's chair.

"What's your name?"

"Emmy Macalik," I said, embarrassed and a little frightened.

"Emmy," he said, gently, "there's nothing for you to laugh at in this scene. Remember that Herr Hörbiger is your father, and that you're in trouble for not having practiced. Can you do that?"

"Yes, sir," I said softly. I was so embarrassed that the thought of giggling at anything seemed quite impossible.

"Test, please!" the man shouted again. Silence came to the set.

Paul Hörbiger again asked Franz why he hadn't practiced, and again Franz replied that he hadn't felt like it, and again Paul Hörbiger asked me why I hadn't practiced. This time I didn't even get as far as "Because" before I collapsed in giggles.

Paul Hörbiger gave his costar a look of mingled outrage and disgust and stormed off the set, swearing under his breath.

There was a round of applause. I looked up at the technicians on the scaffolding. They were smiling from ear to ear and applauding.

Willy Forst walked onto the set.

"Well, Emmy," he said, "you've got my electricians on your side. It takes a good deal to get them to applaud anything. I can't remember their ever having applauded Mr. Hörbiger." There was laughter all over the set.

But then he grew serious. "I'm sorry, Emmy, but time is money here. You go sit on the couch. You won't have to say anything, and we'll get the other girl over here."

So ended my career as a motion picture actress.

The girl who took my place had no problem at all. She acted as naturally as Franz had. After one test the scene was taken by the camera, and Director Forst ordered a print of the second take.

There were two or three other shots on that set, and then we broke for lunch. It wasn't much of a lunch, but it was furnished on the Heavy Workers ration, and it was better than could be had in a restaurant.

I saw Ilse coming into the commissary as we were leaving, and she looked at me curiously, as if she recognized me. She was with a well-dressed man about as old as Herr Forst, and I presumed this was her director. It wasn't the time to walk up to her and say something.

In the afternoon we worked on another set, this time a street with fake trees and a backdrop of small, old-fashioned houses painted on canvas.

I managed my afternoon role without difficulty, since I wasn't required to say anything. All I had to do was walk on a narrow sidewalk with another girl, smile, and make believe that we were happily gossiping.

The next day it was back to school.

I found Ilse's name listed in the telephone book, but when I tried to call her, there was no answer. That could have meant that no one was at home, but more likely that her line was out of order. I would have to wait until I got another summons to Rosenhügel before seeing her.

The next week I went back for two days' work as a member of the chorus in a dance segment. Not ballet, and not quite ballroom dancing either. Just one of a dozen nearly out-of-focus dancers swaying in the background. I didn't get to see Ilse then either. When I asked about her, I was told that she was shooting and that I shouldn't disturb her.

For the next month, I went once or twice a week to Rosenhügel as they made *The Viennese Girls*. I had a few minor dancing roles, in flat shoes, but usually I was an extra in the background.

I was more than happy to be an extra. I had the chance to watch how the movies were made. I was fascinated to see how the bona fide actors could instantly change from being themselves when the camera began to roll and become someone else entirely.

When the cameras were rolling, the actors in their Baroque costumes "living" in the old-fashioned houses seemed so real to me that I felt as if I had entered the world of a century before.

When I got my first check, I felt almost guilty. I was paid, I thought, far too much for what I had done. My first check more than covered two months' tuition at the Conservatorium. When I got my second check, I had nothing to spend it on because there was nothing in the stores. I had to content myself with feeling important when my mother opened an account for me in a bank on Gumpendorferstrasse.

I went to the movies one night, and there was Ilse on the screen. Not in the riding habit I'd seen her wear at the studio, and certainly not in a major role, but up there on the screen, saying her lines like a professional.

And the next time I went to the studios, I saw her. She was sitting alone at a table in the commissary, her fur coat over her shoulders, bent over a script as she drank a cup of tea.

After thinking it over a minute, I walked over and stood by the table and said hello.

"I thought it was you," she said, and got up and hugged me.

She showed me her script, and the lines she was learning, and I helped her with them for an hour or so until it was time for me to go back to my set. She told me that she was working full time at the studios, under contract, and that the next time I was at work and had a moment free, I should look for her in her dressing room.

It was two weeks before I had a chance to take up the invitation. I was an extra on a new film by then, another love story played in fancy costume. Most of the films being made were, as American films in the Great Depression had been, designed to take their audience's minds off their problems. Vicariously living the grand and romantic life of Austro-Hungary's Belle Epoque was the way it was done in Vienna.

Ilse's dressing room was off one of the large sound stages, and I found it without trouble.

I heard voices inside, but there was no response to my knock. I knocked again, and when again there was no response, I decided I hadn't been heard, and I pushed the door open.

Ilse and the middle-aged man I had seen her with that first time in the commissary were in the dressing room. Specifically, they were on a chaise lounge. I had just turned sixteen, and I was a virgin, but sixteen-year-old virgins often know more about the facts of life than their mothers like to think they do.

I knew exactly what Ilse and the middle-aged director were doing on her chaise lounge, even though I don't think I had the door open more than ten seconds, no longer than it took to see them, and to see Ilse's face looking over the director's naked back at me.

Later that day, she came looking for me on my set.

"That's the way things are done around here, Emmy," she said. "And you'd better understand it. Otherwise, you'll never be anything more than an extra."

I couldn't think of anything to say to her, anything at all. After a moment, she shrugged her shoulders, adjusted her fur coat, and walked off the set.

Chapter 17

Working at the Rosenhügel Studios had another very real advantage in addition to the Heavy Workers ration we were given for lunch.

Although the Allies were now bombing Vienna regularly, Rosenhügel, on the distant outskirts of the city, was yet to be bombed.

Some of the bombing attacks were massive, and caused great destruction. Some involved just a dozen aircraft, and were intended primarily to disrupt life in the city. We went to the large and relatively comfortable shelter at Rosenhügel whenever enemy planes obviously bound for Vienna were sighted, whether it was ten medium bombers or five hundred heavy ones.

The "democracy of the shelters" applied at Rosenhügel, too. There were no "stars" or "extras," just people hoping not to be bombed. I often found myself sitting beside one famous actor or actress or another, and they all seemed to go out of their way to be nice to me, asking my name, and, when they learned I was one of the "kids from the ballet," talking about the stars of my profession.

There was another studio, for interiors, downtown in the Inner City, on the top floor of a large modern apartment building. They seldom required extras to work there, but on those few occasions when I was, I was always afraid, for it was on the center of Vienna that most bombs fell.

Then I began to change my mind about that. It was getting more and more difficult to get back and forth to Rosenhügel on the streetcars, and as the intensity of the bombing increased, it no longer seemed to matter where in Vienna you were, for bombs would inevitably fall there, too. I now began to hope that I would be called to the Inner City studios because it would spare me the long ride to Rosenhügel, and, if necessary, I could walk to work, or home, if the bombs knocked out the streetcar tracks.

In order to keep us off balance and frightened, the Allies alternated their "harassing" raids, attacks by just a few bombers that did little relative damage but sent everybody to the shelters and disrupted work in the factories, with "massive" raids. Massive raids involved hundreds of bombers, and inflicted massive damage wherever the bombs fell. Sometimes there was a target (the rail-yards or an industrial area), but sometimes the bombs destroyed a section of the city without apparent reason beyond reminding us of the Allies' awesome military power.

There was little doubt in anyone's mind that a government, no matter how desperate, and military forces, no matter how brave, that could not stop the Allies from bombing day after day whatever target they wanted to hit, was going to have a hard time winning the "Final Victory." But to suggest that Germany had lost the war was treason, and treason was punishable, in "The People's Courts," by death.

In the early months of 1944, on a day I was working at Rosenhügel, the Americans (who bombed in the daytime) launched a massive raid on Vienna. Even in the Rosenhügel shelter, it was possible to determine the general area of Vienna that was taking the beating. This time I knew it was the Sixth Bezirk, and when the thunder of the bombs and the rumble of the antiaircraft stopped and the all-clear siren sounded, I was sick with fear that when I got home, my home and my mother would be gone.

The raid had lasted so long that we were dismissed as soon as we came out of the shelters. Rubble from bombed-out buildings blocked the streetcar tracks close to my neighborhood, and I had to walk the last six or seven blocks. Our apartment building had not been hit, and my mother was waiting for me, as worried about me as I had been about her.

She told me that she had heard there had

been severe damage around Spiegelgasse in the Inner City, and that we should thank God I had been ordered to work at Rosenhügel rather than downtown.

I had been called to Rosenhügel, but three of the "kids from the ballet" had been ordered to the Inner City studios on Spiegelgasse.

I ran out of the apartment and downtown, a distance of about two miles. When I got to Spiegelgasse, there was nothing left of the building but a pile of smoldering rubble.

There was a crowd of people, mostly women, standing nearby. I recognized two of them. They were the mothers of my friends who had gone to work that day at the Inner City studios. They were crying. One woman was screaming.

I felt someone's eyes on me. I turned and saw Willy Forst, the director, wearing a camel's hair coat, standing alone a short distance away from the other people.

I went to him in the hope that he would tell me that my friends had somehow lived through the destruction of the building. But, instead, he put his arm around my shoulders and held me tight. I held myself back for a moment, and then let loose and wept into his coat. Behind me, I heard a man's voice:

"Did she lose a relative?"

"No," Herr Forst told him. "All we've lost are three friends."

They had separate funerals, and most of the "kids from the ballet" showed up for all of them. When we went, out of habit more than anything else, to the Conservatorium, none of us felt like practicing. Sitting around glumly, we agreed that none of us wanted to go to the studio anymore, either.

When Frau Dertl came into the hall, we told her how we felt.

She said she understood our feelings, but told us that life had to go on. It wouldn't do our friends who had died any good if we stopped practicing, and they wouldn't want us to stop doing what we had all loved to do for so long.

We thought that over and, without saying anything, got ready to practice as usual.

When *The Viennese Girls*, the first film we had made, was finished and released, Marcella, Frau Jensen, and my mother and I went to see it. They were all excited to see me on the screen.

I looked all right, I thought, in the pretty costume and wearing the blond wig with long curls. But I realized that the movie business didn't really excite me as much as the ballet did.

In June 1944, the Allies went ashore in Normandy. In a few days, it was evident that they would not be, as Hitler promised, "thrown back into the sea."

Shortly after the Normandy Invasion, while the war was raging on both fronts, the newspapers announced that in tribute to

Maestro Richard Strauss, who was about to celebrate his eightieth birthday, the Opera would reopen long enough to perform three of his operas. He would be there.

When my mother showed me the newspaper, I was delighted. I really wanted to see Maestro Strauss, but when I said so to my mother, she replied, "Don't get your hopes up. I'm sure the tickets were gone before they put the story in the paper."

She was right, of course. Tickets had gone to the influential, and to the Army and the Air Force, and none were for sale. But I knew that dignitaries always went backstage after a performance to greet the leading performers. If I were backstage, I would be able to see him, ticket or no ticket.

The next day during practice I explained to Frau Dertl how I had come to know Richard Strauss. She promptly wrote out a pass for me to be backstage during the performances. She might no longer be in the Opera House, but she was still the ballet mistress.

Standing backstage during the performance, it was almost like the old days. With the artists in costume, and the stagehands, the orchestra in the pit, and the house full, it was easy to forget that outside, many of the buildings on the Ring were bombed-out hollow shells, and that it was entirely likely that the howl of the air raid warning sirens would interrupt the performance.

But the sirens didn't go off. The final curtain fell, and the house once again rang with applause, louder probably than usual because Maestro Strauss was in the Emperor's box.

He came backstage a few minutes later, and when he did, I saw that he was older and thinner, but still had his full head of white hair. He was surrounded by a group of men and women in evening dress. It was as if there was no war.

I pushed myself through the group of people to him. A man standing next to him tried to stop me, but I was already close enough to the Maestro to grab his hand. He turned his head toward me and looked at me without recognition.

"Herr Strauss," I said, suddenly very shy, "it's Emmy. Do you remember me?"

He smiled and took both of my hands in his.

"Emmy!" he said happily. "I didn't recognize you. You've become a young lady."

A woman wearing a glistening diamond necklace and an evening dress started to talk to him.

"Excuse us, please," Herr Strauss said to her icily, and led me a few feet away.

"How are you? Do you still like to dance?"

"Didn't you know?" I said. "I've been in the Corps de Ballet since I was eight."

"Wonderful!" he said. "If only Frau Fischer could see you now."

I asked him about his two friends. He told me they had died. Then the lady with the glistening necklace came over to us and took his arm.

"I must go, Emmy," Maestro Strauss said. I made my curtsy and started to say "Küss die Hand," but Maestro Strauss caught my head in his hands and kissed me on the cheek. Then he was quickly pushed away by the people who surrounded him.

Memories of Tuesday with Frau Fischer came back to me. Memories of the stale cookies and the bitter tea Gertrude had served.

"They are from England, you know," Frau Fischer had used to say, so proudly, about her cookies.

Later that night there was another air raid. What we got now from England was bombs.

I spent most of my waking hours in the summer of 1944 standing in food lines. The lines were four-people wide, and often thirty yards long. While my mother stood in the butcher line, I stood in the grocery line; while she stood in the bakery store line, I stood in the vegetable store line, or the milk store line. What little milk was available was gray and watery, tasted badly, and could only be used for cooking. What little margarine there was tasted like soap. There was, of course, no butter.

Fall came, and the food shortages grew worse. I fainted several times during *barre* exercises at the Conservatorium. I was always hungry and weak, and often felt dizzy. Then I contracted dysentery. The doctor gave me medicine, which "cured" me, but he declared me physically unfit to continue dancing. But that didn't really matter: I was still sick in bed when a letter came from Frau Dertl announcing that classes were suspended until the war was over. "My prayers are with you, Emmy. God bless you," she wrote.

School had changed, too. Even BDM uniforms were in short supply, or unavailable, so the girls with Nazi influence were as shabbily dressed as Marcella and I were.

The clothes we wore reminded me of those the organ grinder who used to come to my courtyard had worn. Patched and cheap, and dirty, because there was no laundry soap either. But at least it wasn't cold yet, and I didn't have to worry about keeping warm.

I was disappointed when school started again in the fall and the teacher said they were "temporarily out" of the daily vitamin pill. Up to then, we had been given, every day, a vitamin pill that was supposed to give us strength. I didn't think that was true, but the sugar-coated pills were the only candy I ever got, and I had been looking forward to them.

Once, when it had been my turn to pick up the tray of vitamins from the office, I stole a handful of the pills and ate them as quickly as I could. Ten minutes later, I developed a terrible stomach cramp and was nauseous. It was worth it to have been able to eat something sweet.

One day, instead of being told to get out our books, we were shown how to prepare cotton face masks such as doctors and nurses wear. Most of us thought they were intended for the hospitals, but when we had finished making them, we were told what they were really for.

Five elderly men wearing steel helmets took us from the classroom to buildings that had been bombed the night before.

While we marched to the bombed-out buildings, we sang. I didn't know whose idea that was. Marcella and I certainly didn't feel like singing. The BDM girls, however, sang enthusiastically. I couldn't understand them. There was no one to watch us now as once there had been on the Ring when we had marched along to the City Park. We were ignored by the few people we met. In our patched clothes, gray or black woolen stockings, and wooden shoes we looked more like poor old women than sixteen-year-old girls.

Some of the bombed buildings we passed had been neatly cut in half, with part of their apartments still recognizable. Furniture and bathtubs (usually upside down) hung over the edges of what once had been somebody's apartment floor.

Debris littered the streets and people searched through it for what possessions might have missed destruction. Most of the time the search was fruitless.

The technology of the bombing had changed. The Americans now dropped incendiary bombs with the high-explosive bombs. Whatever wasn't destroyed by explosives was burned.

At the "site," the elderly men passed out thick cotton work gloves, with a stern admonishment that they would have to be returned when we were finished. (I never found out why we couldn't keep them.) One or two of the men began the job by entering the ruin to look for looters. Looters interrupted at their work often responded with violence.

The unbearable smell of burned human flesh rose from the rubble. The face masks didn't help much. At all. Our job was to dig out dismembered bodies from the ruins. We put them into water buckets. The remains of one body fitted into three buckets.

Several times we dug out pieces of unburned cloth, which people standing around the ruins recognized as belonging to a relative or someone they had known. They wanted someone to blame for the deaths of the friends and relatives. We were there. There was hysterical screaming and often the old men had a hard time protecting us from the frustrated rage of the survivors.

Two of the old men had the job of constantly watching the walls still standing around us. In another part of Vienna, thirty boys and girls doing what we were doing had been killed by a falling wall. After that happened, the authorities issued strict orders to our supervisors to watch the walls.

When a wall cracked and groaned, or when bricks began to fall down from a wall, we were quickly moved to another, "safer," bombed-out building.

There was a one-hour lunch break. We were given a Heavy Workers ration, now reduced to two soggy slices of dark bread covered with a thin layer of margarine and a layer of marmalade made from carrots and saccharin. While we sat eating our lunch in the rubble, the old men tried to cheer us up by telling us jokes. I often thought about my grandfather. He used to tell me jokes, too, and I wondered if he would have let me do what I was ordered to do now.

My mother cried every time I came home, but she couldn't stop me from going. By now, everybody was afraid of the Gestapo, even her.

We seldom got through with a "site" in one day, and we knew that if a wall didn't fall down, we would have to return the next day. And the next. Until we had all the parts of all the bodies.

We worked until two or two-thirty in the afternoon, and then the old man marched us back to school.

I was afraid at night and kept a small lamp burning in my room. It was impossible to get the smell of burned and decomposing flesh out of my nostrils, and I had horrible nightmares: Burned bodies climbed out of the rubble and tried to get me. When I told Marcella about it, she said she had the same problem. She said that when her nightmares woke her up, she prayed. Praying helped her to get back to sleep, she said. I couldn't pray. I hadn't prayed for quite some time because I had stopped believing in God. I told Marcella I envied her faith.

On one "site," I turned over a door in the rubble and uncovered the body of a woman. The body, wearing a flower-print dress, was only half burned.

The smell was horrible, and the sight of the torn, bloody, half-burned body made me sick to my stomach. Some of the vomitus that exploded out of me went on my face and I cleaned it with the face mask. Then I looked around for someone to help me. No one even noticed me. The other girls were bent over, digging for bones; the men were looking up at the walls. I turned back, and was faced again with the woman's body. Across the street, I saw a park.

I backed carefully away from the body and made my way out of the rubble, and then ran across the street into the park. I hid behind one of the large bushes. I felt more vomitus dripping down my chin. When I looked for my face mask, it was gone. I had dropped it by the burned body. I cleaned my chin with the hem of my dress.

A few minutes later, Marcella, frightened because she had lost sight of me, came running into the park calling out my name.

"I'm here," I called quietly from behind the bush.

"What happened, Emmy?" she asked when she had crawled in beside me.

"I can't take this anymore!" I cried. "I just can't."

"Let's go home," Marcella said, putting her arm around my shoulder, "and never come back."

We did. From then on, we stopped going to school. We hid during the day in either Marcella's apartment or mine. The authorities were either too busy to look for us, or thought we had been killed in the bombing.

We killed time at first playing cards, and when we grew bored with that, we taught each other foreign languages. I had studied Latin and English for four years and Marcella had taken Latin and French.

Marcella taught me how to speak through my nose as the French do. I taught her how to pronounce the English *th* by putting the tongue slightly forward, against the teeth, making the sound that to a German-speaking person sounds like stuttering. We laughed a lot, mimicking our teachers. But we studied hard, even giving each other homework and grading each other's work.

I didn't miss school as much as I did the ballet. Frequently, I put on my practice outfit and tried to do the *barre* exercises holding onto the back of a chair. But I could never finish them. I always became weak and faint.

I had lost a great deal of weight, more than even the poor diet should have made me lose. My mother took me to the doctor again. This time, the doctor said I didn't only have a dietary protein deficiency, but something worse. I had developed a bone disease called rickets. The doctor tried to assure my mother that it wasn't serious. It was a painless disease, and many young people had rickets from not having enough of the right kind of food.

He said that I was lucky. I had developed only a slightly sunken rib cage. Rickets in many cases caused grotesquely bowed legs and even worse abnormalities.

A sunken rib cage seemed bad enough to me, and when I got home I went straight to my room. What else was going to happen to me, I wondered, before the war was over? What if the war never did end and everybody starved to death or got killed? Worst of all, my father might already be dead. We hadn't heard from him for a very long time.

Usually, hugging Petja tight, I cried myself to sleep.

Chapter 18

My father, finally given a leave to come home, arrived without warning. When I saw him in his ill-fitting uniform I was shocked. He was very thin, his hair had turned gray, and he looked like an old man. I felt sorry for him, but he was even more upset about what he found at home.

My father said that he had heard about the bombing, had even suspected it had been worse than he had been told, but that he had had no idea how bad things really were.

There wasn't enough food. I had lost my entitlement to Heavy Workers ration coupons when the classes at the Conservatorium had been canceled. My mother and I had ration coupons for coal, but none was available. We wrapped ourselves in blankets to keep warm in the living room at night.

A week before my father came home the Americans had bombed the West railroad station. Five hundred women and children were killed while waiting to get on a train to leave Vienna.

I asked my father why the Allies had done such a terrible thing if they were really, as the BBC said, our friends, and opposed only to the Nazis in power. He told me it could have been a mistake. Sometimes, he said, the Germans killed their own people by mistake, too.

I was very frightened by all the bombing and for a long time had wanted to get out of Vienna. My mother refused to even consider it. Now that my father was home, I begged him to talk her into leaving, to let us go to the country as so many others were doing.

"You can't run away from your destiny, Emmy," he told me. "One never knows what can happen in a strange place. We must leave things up to God."

I wished that he would have left God out of the argument. I had been thinking a lot about God lately, wondering why He permitted all the misery. I had stopped going to church, and couldn't remember when I had last gone to Confession or taken Communion. I had nothing to confess except being afraid, and the priest couldn't help me with that, so I had simply stopped going. But my father still had his faith and I couldn't tell him about how I felt about God and the Holy Roman Catholic Church.

The inevitable air raid came while I was making a cake for him. As I stood by the kitchen window kneading gray flour, carrots, saccharin, and my weekly ration of one small egg, the siren began its shrill wailing.

My father didn't want to go to the shelter in the basement. He said that there weren't any shelters where he had been. My mother and I had to force him to go. Just as we reached the cellar door there was a horrible explosion. The walls and floors of the building shook. I was sure that our building had finally been hit, and was terrified with the knowledge that if our apartment was bombed out, we had no place to go. My father saw how upset I was and hugged me, and then led us into the shelter.

When the all-clear siren blew and we went back upstairs, we saw that the apartment house immediately behind our building had been hit. There was little left but a huge bomb crater, one wall, and a pile of rubble.

Although our building hadn't been seriously damaged, glass splinters from our blown-out kitchen windows had fallen into the cake batter I had been making for my father. I didn't have any more carrots or another egg. I couldn't make him another cake, and I cried.

Sometime later that night, my father and I were alone for a moment in the living room.

"I want you to have this," he said sadly, handing me a large revolver with shaking hands. "It's loaded. Be very careful. It's dangerous, but it's the only thing I can think of doing for you." Then he thought of my mother. "We can't leave it here," he said. "It would worry your mother. We'll hide it in the coal cellar."

The only gun I had ever touched before was my father's hunting shotgun. Before the war, he had brought home a lot of ducks and rabbits. The revolver was ugly and I was afraid of it. My father wrapped it in a large piece of cloth, and then we went downstairs and hid it in the coal bin.

"Take it out only if you are in great danger," he told me. "I know that the Germans are going to lose the war, and I'm afraid that the Russians are going to take Vienna. If you need it, you must pull the trigger right away. Do you understand me?" His face looked very worried. I nodded. "And don't let your mother or anybody else know about it."

I nodded my head again, in agreement, somehow proud that my father had trusted me, instead of my mother, with the revolver. I didn't like what he said about the Russians coming to Vienna, and I wasn't sure that I really believed him. I went to the movies regularly, and saw one German victory after another in the newsreels, and heard about German victories every day on Radio Vienna. And even if the Germans lost the war, I thought, the Americans and the English, not the Russians, would come to Vienna, and to help, not to do the horrible things we heard the Russians would do.

The next day, my father took me with him to visit his father. My grandfather had been sick and my Aunt Anna had been taking care of him. My father bought him a bottle of wine. The old man fell asleep after the second glass. He looked very old and weak. But I felt more sorry for my father: He seemed so very sad, sitting thoughtfully next to Grandfather's bed holding his hand. My father looked silently at his father for a long time, then he kissed him on the forehead, stood up, and led me into the living room.

My aunt told us that she had sent my cousins Trudy and Hilde to the country where they would be safe from the bombing. Uncle Hubert would have wanted it that way, she said. Uncle Hubert had been captured with the Afrika Korps. Uncle Otto was in Russia.

I knew how my father felt about my leaving Vienna, but he didn't say anything. He changed the subject and asked his sister about her son, my cousin Fritz. He was doing great, Aunt Anna said proudly. He had been given command of a fighter squadron, been promoted to captain, and received the Knight's Cross to the Iron Cross.

I suddenly was filled with bitterness toward Fritz, too. He was one of those who loved the uniforms and the medals of war. But it was people like Olaf who got killed.

Outwardly, my father was as nice as he had ever been to Aunt Anna, but I saw their relationship was changed. He was like a stranger being nice to another stranger.

My mother told Aunt Anna to let her know

if there was anything she could do for my grandfather. My aunt thanked her and said that he wasn't really sick, he was just lonesome and getting old. He had never gotten over missing Grandmother.

I was glad when we could leave. It was all too sad, and I was uncomfortable around my aunt, who was still wearing the Nazi pin.

The next day we took my father to the railroad station again. Much had changed, I realized, since the first time we had taken him there. The war had made me grow up. Now I didn't know who would get killed. When I kissed my father good-bye, I whispered into his ear that I wouldn't forget what he had told me to do. He nodded his head and held me tight.

"God bless you!" he said. I knew that he understood.

Christmas of 1944, the sixth Christmas of the war, passed by almost without notice. My mother and I made the traditional required visit to see my grandfather. The once-pleasant, half-hour streetcar trip across Vienna was now a three-hour ordeal. There were few streetcars now. Their heaters had been shut off to conserve electricity, and their windows were painted over. They were jammed full of people, none of whom had had either the soap or the hot water for a good bath in a long time.

The route was determined by the enemy. The streetcar had to carry its cargo of cold, disheartened, poorly clothed, and badly smelling passengers where there were still tracks, around areas where the tracks had been blown up and not yet relaid, or areas that had their streets blocked by rubble.

When we got to my grandfather's house, he was in bed. Aunt Anna, who had been forced to give up her apartment to house bombed-out people, had moved in with him. She told us Uncle Otto was still in Russia and that there had been another letter from Uncle Hubert, who was in a prisoner-of-war camp in Texas, in America. She told us she was glad we had come; Grandfather hadn't smiled for a long time.

I understood that. My mother and I hadn't smiled for a long time either. Life had become more and more unbearable, and our morale was low, despite the constant, almost frenzied effort of the government to convince us things weren't as bad as they seemed and would soon get better anyway.

We no longer believed what we read in the newspapers, or heard on the radio, or saw in the movie newsreels.

The only propaganda that kept us going was British. We regularly listened to the BBC. Doing so twice violated the law. Radios capable of being tuned to the BBC or other non-German-controlled stations had been ordered turned in early in the war. Possession alone of such a radio was a "grave" offense. Listening to the BBC was a separate, even more grave offense, which approached treason in the eyes of the Nazis.

The government had made available from the early days of the Nazi reign a cheap, fixed-frequency radio, which received only stations under German control. My parents had kept our multiband radio in defiance of the law because they believed that being able to get news from outside of Germany was worth the risk.

My parents trusted me to keep my mouth shut about it, and I was permitted to listen, too.

The British Broadcasting Corporation's "London Calling" told us that the German Army was losing, and we believed that, and when the BBC said that the Germans were retreating on all fronts, we believed that, too. But the most important thing the BBC had to say was, "Don't despair! Help is coming!"

I know now that that was just a propaganda technique going back to the Romans — "Divide and Conquer" — but it worked. It was easy to like hearing that the bombs falling on us weren't intended for us, but for the Nazis, and that the English and the Americans really didn't hate the Viennese, just those Viennese who were Nazis.

But then we lost even that faint reassurance. A young woman in the building next to ours, whose husband was missing in Russia, had been turned in by a zealous Nazi neighbor for listening to the BBC. The Gestapo came on Christmas Day and took her and her two small children away. After that, we were afraid to listen to the "enemy" broadcasts.

Two days after Christmas, a postcard came from my father. There had been no mail from him for some time. It was a printed form. It gave his name and number and the information that he had been captured and was imprisoned in France. At least, I thought with enormous relief, he was alive and safe!

My mother tried to call my grandfather with the news, but the telephone lines were out. They were out most of the time now. We decided we had to go back across Vienna to tell him in person.

Aunt Anna arrived at our apartment just as my mother and I were about to leave. She had news, too, that she hadn't been able to telephone.

Grandfather was dead. He had just gone to sleep and never awakened.

At his funeral, I broke down. Not only because of my grandfather's death — I had expected that for some time — nor even because my father couldn't be with us. Just because there seemed nothing left.

Three days after we buried my grandfather, Aunt Anna came unexpectantly again, and again with bad news: Fritz had been killed.

He had died the way he would have wanted to, she said, in his Messerschmidt fighter plane. He had gone up with his squadron to attack a wave of American bombers. The American bombers were now accompanied by their own fighter planes. The officer from the Luftwaffe had told my aunt there had been a dog fight. The American fighter pilot had been more skilled than Fritz, or luckier.

Fritz had gone down. They had not recovered the body, so there would be no funeral. Just his name in the daily "Fallen for the Fatherland" listing in the newspaper.

I felt very sorry for Aunt Anna, of course. And I was sorry that Fritz was dead. But before he had died, he had sent other young men to their deaths, and their mothers had mourned them, too. All that senseless killing! For what?

I couldn't cry, and was glad when Aunt Anna left.

New Year's Day 1945 passed as unnoticed as Christmas had. The chimney sweepers hadn't been to the apartment building in years. There hadn't been coal enough to make the chimneys dirty. We wouldn't have believed that they could bring good luck anyway. We had had war for so long now that we had become numb about good luck.

We took our pleasure in strange things: We were glad that we were now being bombed by the British and Russians instead of the Americans. The British and the Russian bombs didn't seem to do nearly as much damage as the American five-hundred-pound bombs did.

But that didn't last long either. The American B17s came back in March.

They used St. Stephen's Cathedral as the aiming point for a bombing run on the Inner City. The Germans had destroyed the cathedral at Coventry. Now it was Vienna's turn.

When the all-clear sounded, I went to see the damage. I had to walk. The streetcars would not be running for a while, not until after the rubble was cleared from the tracks and the electric wires could be restrung.

When I got to the Ring and started toward Kärntnerstrasse, many of the buildings were still on fire, and firemen were fighting the flames.

The building on the corner of Karntnerstrasse and the Ring had been damaged so severely that the firemen didn't even try to save it. Emperor Franz Joseph's Imperial and Royal Opera House, my second home, was gone, bombed into a smoldering empty shell.

I made my way down Karntnerstrasse. St. Stephen's Cathedral was gone, too. The twenty-ton *Pummerin* bell, which had rung for my confirmation, had crashed onto the cathedral's floor when the bell tower burned.

Chapter 19

The long-anticipated, often-rumored news
that the Russians were approaching Vienna
was confirmed in March of 1945, when the
authorities, making it official, announced
even more emergency rules, and began to
draft young boys and old men into the *Volksturm* (literally, "the people's force") to
"beat back the savages from the gates of
Vienna." We had heard horrifying things
about what the Russians did to civilians,
heard too many things and heard them too
often to dismiss them as propaganda.

The stores were all closed now. Except for
the *Waffen-SS* (the armed branch of the
Schutzstaffel), out looking for deserters and
draft-dodgers, there was hardly anybody on
the streets.

One afternoon the doorbell rang and
wouldn't stop ringing. I was afraid to answer
it. For all I knew it was the Russians, literally at my door. But when I finally gathered

my courage and opened the door, it was only Marcella, white and shocked.

She told me that while she was taking Max, Olaf's German shepherd, for a walk on Mittelgasse, near her apartment, two men had grabbed him and run off with him. Marcella had run after them, but she couldn't keep up and they got away. We had heard, and had been unable to dismiss the rumor, that people were stealing dogs and cats for food.

Two days after that, when Marcella was again in the apartment, there were shouting, hammering, and other strange noises on Gumpendorferstrasse. When we looked out, we saw that horse-drawn artillery was being set up in front of our building. German soldiers were taking shells from wooden crates. Their horses were tied to the lamp poles on the street.

A few minutes later, Frau Jensen burst in to take Marcella home wtih her. But the German soldiers wouldn't let them back onto the street. Russian troops were expected any moment, and the fighting was about to begin.

Marcella and I were torn between terror and joy that the war was finally going to be over. We were now almost seventeen. We had been talking about "after the war" since we were ten years old. We had talked about what we wanted most after the war: *Wiener Schnitzel* (Viennese veal cutlet). Not one. Ten! And chocolate cake dripping with butter cream. And leather shoes. And pretty dresses.

But "after the war" seemed still far in the future when soldiers came into the apartment with sandbags, boxes of ammunition, and a machine gun. They told my mother they were going to set it up in our front window so it could be fired down Gumpendorferstrasse. My mother ran frantically to find their officer, and hysterically begged him to find some place else for the machine gun. Finally the soldiers took it away, to put it in somebody else's living room window. The officer stayed behind long enough to tell my mother to hide Marcella and me when the Russians came.

"God bless you," he said, and then he left.

We went to the basement. Frau Müller and Lotte were already there, and they had a problem. Their coal bin was already occupied. The Housing Authority took care of people who had been bombed out by assigning them to whomever had extra rooms. The Müller apartment (formerly the Spinats') was large. Captain Müller was off with the Army. Frau Müller had been ordered to take in bombed-out people, and the bombed-out people who had taken over the Müller coal bin now refused to let the Müllers in.

We took Lotte and her mother in with us. And a half hour later, Marcella's mother came down the stairs. We began to make the necessary arrangements. Lotte and her mother would share one cot. Marcella and I would share my cot. Frau Jensen would have to make do with my father's rocking chair;

my mother's cot was not large enough for both of them. We were almost out of food, and what little we had we obviously would have to share with Marcella and her mother. We had a few cooked, cold potatoes; a soggy loaf of black bread, and a cup or two of cold, dried beans so tiny that we were hungry immediately after we ate them.

My mother urged us to try to sleep. Asleep, we wouldn't feel our hunger. Incredibly enough, we could sleep.

Artillery fire woke me and I whispered to Marcella, "Are you asleep?"

"I was," she replied unhappily. "Go back to sleep."

"I can't," I said.

"If you pray long enough, you can go to sleep," Marcella said firmly.

"I can't pray," I said firmly. "I don't believe there is a God."

"You're wrong, Emmy," she replied confidently. "And God is going to help you no matter how you feel about Him."

I didn't say anything. I envied her. I pulled my blanket over my head, pressed my fists to my stomach so it wouldn't hurt so much, and finally went to sleep, without praying.

When I woke up again, light was coming through the narrow windows by the ceiling. The cannon in front of the building was firing, and there was the crackling of rifle and machine-gun fire, too. I could see the boots of soldiers running back and forth on the sidewalk. Would this be the day, I wondered, when the war would be over?

For breakfast we had a half slice of bread, three small spoonfuls of beans, and a couple of chunks of cold potatoes.

I had my playing cards, and Lotte, Marcella, and I played rummy. When our legs became stiff from sitting in the same position, we went into the narrow passageway between the coal bins and exercised by running in place.

Finally, the artillery firing slowed and then stopped all together. My mother looked out the tiny windows and reported the cannon was deserted.

"I guess," she said finally, "that it's all over now. I'll go and take a look." Frau Jenson followed her.

They were gone only a few minutes, but I was terribly afraid that something awful would happen to my mother, and I was enormously relieved when, a few minutes later, they returned.

"The Russians are here!" my mother whispered.

Frau Müller and Frau Jensen began to weep. I didn't. I was just relieved that my mother had returned. Nothing else seemed to matter.

My mother told Frau Müller what the German officer had said about hiding us girls when the Russians came. What did Frau Müller plan to do with Lotte?

Frau Müller became hysterical. Her twins, the fourteen-year-old boys, she howled, had been taken off into the *Volksturm*. She complained bitterly that she had no idea where the boys were, or where her husband was, and now she had to worry about her daughter, too!

My mother calmed her down by telling her she would take care of Lotte with Marcella and me. But she also told her that if she had some food hidden somewhere, now was the time to get it. Frau Müller went up the stairs to her apartment.

Our bin was the most remote from the cellar door of the coal bins and my mother decided it would be the best place for us to hide from the Russians. We took furniture from other bins and arranged it in such a way that nobody could see us if we hid behind it. My mother gave us candles and matches, and ordered us to blow them out the moment we heard a noise on the cellar stairs, even if it was her voice. Shaking with fear, we nodded our understanding.

Frau Müller returned with a big basket full of salami, sardines, and chocolate. The Nazis still had food we hadn't seen for years. There were even a bag of coffee beans, cans of condensed milk, and even real sugar cubes.

Lotte, Marcella, and I stayed in the coal bin alone that night and all the next day. I had my father's pistol, which had been hidden all along in the coal bin. If anything should go wrong, I thought, I knew what to do. I wasn't afraid of the pistol anymore.

The pistol was not to be used on the Russians. My father had not spelled it out for me, but I knew what it was for. It was for me, if I decided that it would be better to die by my own hand than to be raped by half a dozen Russians and then, probably, killed anyway.

Two or three Russian soldiers came into the basement late the second night. It was dark and they didn't look into the last coal bin. All the time they were in the basement, I had my hand on my father's pistol. I don't know what I would have done if they had found us.

When we were sure the Russians were gone, we hugged and kissed each other in the dark and cried with relief that we hadn't been discovered.

Several hours after the Russians left, just as it was growing light, I heard my mother's voice at the basement steps. She called out that it was all right to light the candle again, and to come out from our hiding place.

Frau Müller took Lotte to their apartment and Marcella and I went to my apartment.

I was so happy to be safe in my apartment that I didn't at first notice my mother's strange behavior. She cried and held me tight. I thought perhaps she had finally stopped being the strong person she was, and that she was crying with relief we hadn't been found by the Russians. But that wasn't why she was crying.

My mother had taken Petja with her to the apartment so that his barking in the basement wouldn't give us away. Petja had barked at the Russian soldiers who searched our apartment and one of them had crushed his skull with a rifle butt.

At first, we were afraid to leave the building. Through the somehow still intact glass in the lobby door, we could see the dead Russian and German soldiers, and the dead civilians, men and women. They were lying on the street among the dead horses. Downed electric wires had electrocuted many of the humans. They were blue black. Marcella and I vomited.

Three days later we ran out of food. We had to leave the building now to search for food or starve. When we pushed open the door, the dead Russians were gone from Gumpendorferstrasse, but the German soldiers and civilians and the horses, now grotesquely swollen and smelling of decay, were still lying on the street.

We stepped carefully between the dead people and horses. But my wooden shoes slipped on the slimy street and I fell onto a rotten horse. I screamed. A White Russian officer heard me, and ran to me.

He picked me up and carried me to the far sidewalk. He cleaned my hands of the putrid slime with his handkerchief. When I thanked him, he smiled at me.

We found a store on Mariahilferstrasse where food was being distributed, and got in line. After we had been standing in the warm spring sun for perhaps three hours, two Russian soldiers approached us. They were Mongolians, about five feet tall, their heads shaven, dressed in quilted uniforms. They looked savage, and I was afraid of them.

One Mongolian soldier walked by us, but the other one grabbed my wrist. I was too terrified to scream. Then, as quickly as he had grabbed it, he let loose of my wrist and went away.

After we got the food ration, maybe an hour later, I looked at my wrist to see what time it was. The watch was gone. That's what the Mongolian had been doing with my wrist. He had stolen my confirmation watch.

People slowly began to appear on the streets again, but only in the daytime. At night there was curfew. European Russian officers roamed the streets. When they came across a Mongolian robbing or raping a civilian, they shot him on the spot. But there weren't enough White Russian officers, or military policemen, to control all the Asiatics.

On the second Sunday "after the war was over," my mother and I went to surprise Frau Jensen and Marcella with an "afternoon coffee." I had ground up the coffee beans Frau Müller had given us, and we took with us a can of her condensed milk and some of her real sugar cubes. We would have no cake for our afternoon coffee, but we would have some of Frau Müller's Nazi chocolate.

On the way to the Jensens' apartment, we passed the bank on Gumpendorferstrasse where I had my account. The doors were wide open, and we heard excited voices inside.

Then half a dozen women and one old man came out carrying stacks of currency. Screaming hysterically, they ran to the middle of the street and threw the money up into the air like so much confetti. Then, they quickly returned into the bank to do the same thing over again.

The street and streetcar tracks were soon covered with money. People stood around, either watching or stepping on the money or picking it up and tearing it into small pieces.

I asked my mother what was going on. She said our money wasn't worth anything anymore. Knowing that had driven these people crazy.

I had made plans for what I was going to buy with my money when rationing was finally over, and now that plan, too, had been destroyed.

But I had been disappointed so many times in the past that losing my money was just one more inconvenience. I decided I wouldn't let it interfere with our end-of-the-war celebration with Marcella and her mother.

Drinking real coffee out of dainty china cups and eating real chocolate made it seem possible that Vienna would become Vienna again.

Our party was interrupted by the sound of gun shots and people screaming. We ran to the front windows to look.

Six women were running down the street, with a flock of children running after them. Two of the women carried a large, rolled-up rug, so heavy that they kept dropping it. The others carried huge bags. Even the children were loaded down. They were looters.

Twenty feet behind them walked four Russian soldiers, laughing as they fired their machine pistols at the women's feet. The women jumped back and forth, and up and down, screaming in fear, but refused to drop their loot.

The Russians did not shoot at the children, but when the bullets came too close, the children dropped their bags and began to run. The women finally gave up, too, and ran after their children, reluctantly leaving their loot in the middle of the street. The law, German and Russian, was that looters were to be shot on sight. Those women were lucky, I thought.

The soldiers stopped shooting, kicked at the bags and the rug, found nothing they wanted, and then turned and walked away.

When everything was quiet again, Marcella and I sneaked out to see what the looters had left behind.

Frau Jensen and my mother were at first furious when we returned with a bag. But after they saw what it held — expensive silk material with a dainty flower print — they stopped shouting. Frau Jensen later made a dress out of the silk material for Marcella, and my mother made one, nearly identical, for me.

Eventually, the day came when I told my mother that I wanted to go to the Conservatorium to find out when ballet classes would start again. With great reluctance, she permitted me to leave the apartment alone.

When I got off the streetcar at the Ring, I saw Sissy Gruber getting off a streetcar coming from the opposite direction.

We ran to each other, hugged, kissed, and cried for joy. She said that her family had been bombed out, but they were all all right. They were living with relatives. Her father and brother were missing in Russia.

Sissy and I left the Ring and walked down a side street, taking a short cut to the Conservatorium. We saw Russian soldiers — not Mongolians — beside a large truck with a tarpaulin top. We started to walk past them, averting our eyes. I was grabbed from behind. I screamed. I heard Sissy screaming, too. We were dragged to the truck and thrown into the back.

There were five women and one girl our

age already in the truck. I saw that the girl was as afraid as Sissy and I were.

One of the poorly dressed and tough-looking women pointed with a reassuring smile for me to sit down next to her. When I sat down with Sissy on my other side, the woman gently touched my hand. I could feel the callouses of a hard-working woman.

The truck began to move. The two soldiers who had thrown Sissy and me onto the truck sat on the ends of the benches, holding their rifles between their legs.

About ten minutes later, I could feel a sudden lurch as if the truck had rolled over a pile of rubble. I thought nothing of it until a woman sitting next to a plastic window looked out the window and then began to scream: "They just ran over an old man!"

One of the soldiers in the rear got halfway up and gestured threateningly with his rifle, ordering the woman to stop her screaming. The truck didn't even slow down.

I pressed my arms against my stomach so I wouldn't vomit.

What kind of animals were these Russians? What did they want with us? Where were they taking us?

When I had a chance, I asked the woman next to me to ask the woman sitting by the window if she could tell where we were.

"On the outskirts of Vienna, going south," she replied, almost calmly.

I realized that if anything was to be done to get us out of the truck, I was going to have to do it, and I was going to have to do something now.

I remembered I had a nail file in my purse. When I was sure the soldiers weren't looking at me, I put my arms behind my back and stuck the nail file into the tarpaulin. I was going to try to cut a hole large enough for my mouth. When I had, I would scream for help. People would hear me, stop the truck, and get us all out. It would all happen so quickly, I decided, that the soldiers couldn't stop me.

But after I had pushed my nail file into the tarpaulin, I could not tear the heavy canvas, no matter how hard I tried. I realized finally that it was all in vain. It would take a sharp knife to cut through the tough tarpaulin. I cried when I thought that my mother was expecting me home right about then.

And there was no hope of jumping out of the truck. The soldiers with the rifles were obviously prepared to use them if one of us tried to run away. The thought that they would shoot frightened me so much that my hands began to sweat again. I took Sissy's hand and held it tight. At least we were together, I thought.

The truck hurtled on for several hours. I knew that we were now far from Vienna. My body ached from being constantly bounced back and forth. The woman sitting by the window kept looking out of it; everybody else just stared at one another or into space.

Then the woman by the window whispered, "We must be close to the Hungarian border!"

Shortly afterward, the truck stopped. The two soldiers jumped off the truck, opened the tarpaulin, and gestured for us to get off. We found ourselves outside a large farmhouse in the flat countryside near the Hungarian border. A dozen or so dirty-looking European Russian soldiers walked slowly around and examined us as if we were cattle. Or slaves.

We were taken into the farmhouse kitchen, where we were greeted by three tough-looking, middle-aged Austrian women. One of them, who spoke in the slang of the Vienna slums, told us that they had been there a week. She said she couldn't remember when she had eaten as well as she was eating now.

Sissy and I and the other girl from the truck were put to work washing vegetables and peeling potatoes. The women from my group were put to work washing laundry in a cauldron over an open fire.

While we were preparing the vegetables, the other girl from the truck told us her name was Gerta Berger and that she had also been on her way to the Conservatorium when the Russians kidnapped her. Like us, she had wanted to find out when she could go back to school. The Conservatorium now seemed very far away.

After the Russians were fed, we were given their leftovers. It was more food than I had seen in a very long time, and I ate it hungrily, even though I knew that, since it was not an Army ration, it had been taken away from other Austrians.

I saw that the tough-looking slum woman who was so happy with the food had been appointed as sort of an overseer over us by the Russians. She seemed perfectly happy with her new-found importance.

After Sissy, Gerta, and I had cleaned up the kitchen to her satisfaction, she led us to a bedroom over the kitchen. The dresser with the mirror was still there, but there was no bed. Three soiled and torn mattresses had been placed on the floor with dirty, brown, thin blankets lying on top of them.

Our overseer told us not to leave the room until she came for us the next morning. Then she left, closing the door behind her. She didn't lock it, but that wasn't necessary. The stairway down led only to the kitchen.

For the first time we felt safe to talk.

"What are we going to do?" Gerta cried. "My mother will go insane when I don't come home."

"Mine, too," Sissy and I said, together.

I remembered the daily announcements over Radio Vienna of the names and descriptions of people who were missing. I always wondered how these people had disappeared. Now I knew, and I knew that my mother would put my name and description on the radio, too.

"We have to get away from here!" I announced, with far more conviction than I felt.

"How?" Sissy replied despondently. "Russian soldiers are all over."

"We'll just have to wait for a chance, and then run," I said.

"Not tonight," Sissy whispered. "It's too dark. We wouldn't know where to run."

"Anywhere," I said, trying to sound sure of myself. "We'll run away the moment it gets light."

"We can't," Gerta cried. "The Russians will shoot us."

"That's up to you," I replied coldly. "Stay if you want. I'm going."

Finally, too tired to talk anymore, we lay down on the dirty mattresses without even taking off our shoes, and pulled the dirty blankets over us.

We could hear the Russian soldiers singing, but we were so tired, first from fear and then from working so long in the kitchen, that we went to sleep anyway.

I don't know how long we had been asleep when the door to our room was opened and the room flooded with light from hissing gasoline lanterns. Three soldiers in soiled uniforms, laughing loudly, crashed into our room.

Gerta, Sissy, and I sat up on our mattresses and looked with terror at them. I wanted to get up and run away, but one of the soldiers pushed me back on my mattress, put his wrist across my throat, and started to tear my clothes off.

Sissy and Gerta screamed, but I didn't. I

was numb with fear. The smell of the soldier's dirty uniform and unwashed body, mixed with the smell of the alcohol on his breath, made me sick to my stomach.

When he was finished with me and putting his uniform back on, I lay motionless, with my eyes closed. I could hear Sissy and Gerta moaning.

When the Russians finally left us, I got up from the mattress. I felt dizzy, but made my way to the window and opened it. In the moonlight, I saw a stand of trees across a field. The trees were maybe two hundred yards away. I saw no Russian soldiers, but heard a dog barking somewhere.

I made up my mind that I was going now. I didn't care what a risk that might entail. It couldn't be any worse than what had already happened.

The moon went behind a cloud and the field turned dark.

I went to Sissy.

"The next time the moon goes behind a cloud," I said, "I'm going to jump out the window and run through the field to the woods."

"I thought," Sissy said almost dreamingly, "we were going to wait until the morning."

"I'm not going," Gerta said. "They'll kill us."

"I'll go, Emmy," Sissy whispered, and got up from the mattress and tried to fasten her torn blouse.

I turned back to the window and waited for the moon to go behind a cloud. It took a long time. I began to shiver all over from fear. Sissy gripped my hand, holding it so tightly that it hurt.

Eventually, the moon disappeared and it was dark.

I backed onto the window ledge, lowered myself as far as I could, and then let go. I scraped my face and legs on the wall as I fell, and landed so hard that I lost my breath. But nothing was broken. I looked up and saw Sissy's legs coming out of the window.

As I started to run across the field, I heard her fall where I had landed; then, faintly, I could hear her steps behind me.

The moon began to come out from behind the clouds when we were halfway across the field.

I ran even faster. Then I became aware that I could no longer hear Sissy's panting breath behind me. I turned to see where she was.

She was at least twenty yards behind.

"Run faster, Sissy!" I called, as loudly as I dared. The next instant I heard gunfire, two shots, and then I saw Sissy fall. She didn't make any sound at all.

"Get up, Sissy!" I screamed. "Get up!"

She didn't. I started to run again, still screaming at her to get up.

I reached the end of the field and then ran into the woods. Finally, I felt it was safe to turn around. Russian soldiers were bent over Sissy. I watched them pick her up and carry her toward the farmhouse.

Afraid that one of them might have seen me and come after me, I ran farther into the woods, falling and running into limbs in the darkness. I found myself on a road, but was afraid to stay on it, and I ran into the field on the other side. And then through that field. And the field beyond that one.

Possibly an hour later, I saw lights ahead. Exhausted, no longer caring, I dragged myself toward the light. When I got close, I saw that it was coming from a farmhouse.

A dog barked.

A tall man came out of the house. He didn't look like a Russian soldier, and then he said something in German to the dog. The dog ran toward me, sniffed me suspiciously, and then licked my hand and waved his tail.

The man came up. Without saying a word, he took me to his house and called to his wife. A nice-looking woman with a frightened face came down the stairs.

"Don't worry," he said to her. "It's just a girl, running away from the Russians."

I told them I had been kidnapped in Vienna, and that I had no idea where I was.

The woman gave me a glass of milk. I couldn't remember when I had last had real milk, and asked for more. I drank the second glass of milk, and then I vomited. My stomach wasn't used to rich milk.

The next morning the farmer took me back

to Vienna in his horse-drawn cart. It took us two days. The Russians had taken us about two hundred kilometers in their truck.

I didn't tell my mother that I had been raped, but she sensed what had happened and took me to the doctor.

His examination of me was perfunctory. Raped sixteen-year-old girls in Vienna in March of 1945 were as common as the cold.

Chapter 20

The Mongolian Assault Troops were gradually moved out of Vienna and replaced by European Russians. They were more disciplined and less rapacious than the assault troops, and it gradually became safe to go out again.

Six weeks after Sissy was killed, I was on a streetcar on the Ring, returning from another long search for food. The streetcar windows were still painted over, but I had scratched enough paint off my window to be able to see out.

The streetcar stopped at Kärntnerstrasse. The fire-blackened shell of the Imperial and Royal Vienna State Opera House was standing beside the relatively untouched Hotel Bristol.

There was something new at the Bristol. The red flag with the hammer and sickle that had replaced the red flag with the swastika had itself been replaced. A red-and-white striped flag with a blue field of white stars hung from the pole on Kärntnerstrasse.

The Americans had come.

I looked at them as they watched Austrian workmen carrying their luggage and equipment into the hotel. They were as strange as creatures from outer space.

They were in well-fitting, immaculate uniforms. They had their sharply creased trousers tucked in the tops of glistening boots. They wore shirts and neckties, and funny little hats cocked over their eyes.

On their breasts, they wore little silver angel's wings, the insignia of the elite American forces, the paratroops. They were clean-shaven, well-fed, enormous, and seemed to be having a marvelous time.

The streetcar finally moved on.

Epilogue

I had no way of knowing at the time, of course, but when I saw the American paratroopers looking at my burned-out Opera House, I was looking at my past and at my future:

I was to come to know a paratrooper, who promptly proposed marriage although he wasn't any older than I was.

The odds against a marriage between a teen-aged Roman Catholic Viennese ballet dancer and a teen-aged Protestant American paratrooper with no education, no money, and no plans except a vague notion that he might like to be a writer, literally had our families in tears.

His best buddy drove a Jeep two hundred miles through a blizzard to plead with him not to marry me. But he would not be dissuaded, and neither would I.

We were married by a judge of the Austrian Supreme Court, in a ceremony of which the groom understood not one word.

Our marriage is in its fourth decade. It has produced three children. Our daughter Patricia is a journalist on the Birmingham (Alabama) *News*. Last June, she was married to a reporter, Tom Black, she met at work. Our son Bill is a journalist on the Dallas (Texas) *Morning News*. Our son John, sixteen, learned something about the family trade by typing the final manuscript of this book. I say the "family trade" because my husband beat the odds against becoming a writer, too. He has published (and I have retyped) more than 150 books.

There wasn't much I could do when they all ganged up on me and insisted that I had to sit down and commit to paper the story of a little girl in Vienna who long ago and far away wanted to become a dancer.

The Vienna State Opera House was rebuilt and opened again in 1955 with the performance of Beethoven's *Fidelio*. There weren't enough tickets, and the Viennese stood on the Ringstrasse and wept as the opera was broadcast from loudspeakers at every corner for many blocks.

St. Stephen's Cathedral rose again through the determination of the Viennese and with gifts from people from all over the world.

Uncle Otto was reported missing in Russia and is presumed dead.

Uncle Hubert returned from prison camp in the United States shortly after the war, and remarried.

Aunt Anna lived alone with her nieces

until Trudy and Hilde were married. Then she moved into an orphanage and raised the children who were born to Austrian mothers and soldiers of the Army of Occupation.

Marcella became an electronics engineer. She still lives in the same apartment, with her mother. She never married and her mother never remarried.

Herr Jensen returned to Sweden.

Lotte Müller married a British officer and moved with her mother to England. Her father and two brothers never returned from the war.

Richard Strauss died in 1949.

Frau Dertl went into retirement.

Herr Schnitzer died of old age in 1947.

Willy Forst and Paul Hörbiger died in 1981.

My father returned from prison camp in France. In early 1946, he killed himself with the revolver he had given me during the war.

My mother lived with me in the United States, and died of cancer in 1971.

Fairhope, Alabama
Christmas Day 1981

About the Author

Emma Macalik Butterworth was born and educated in Vienna, where she became a student with the Corps de Ballet of the Vienna State Opera at the age of eight. She remained with the Corps de Ballet, ultimately as a dancer, until the Opera was destroyed during World War II. An American citizen for more than a quarter of a century, she is married to a writer. They have three children. A well known engrosser-illuminator whose works hang, among other places, in the United States Senate Office Building, she is also the author of *The Complete Book of Calligraphy*. Emma Macalik Butterworth and her husband live in Fairhope, Alabama.